I Escape!

I Escape!

The Great War's Most Remarkable PoW

J. L. Hardy

Pen & Sword
MILITARY

First published in Great Britain in 2014 by
Pen & Sword Military
an imprint of
Pen & Sword Books Ltd
47 Church Street
Barnsley
South Yorkshire
S70 2AS

ISBN 978 1 47382 376 1

The Publishers have made every effort to trace the author, his estate
and his agent without success and they would be interested to hear
from anyone who is able to provide them with this information.

A CIP catalogue record for this book is available from the British
Library

Typeset in Ehrhardt by
Mac Style Ltd, Bridlington, East Yorkshire
Printed and bound in the UK by CPI Group (UK) Ltd, Croydon,
CRO 4YY

Pen & Sword Books Ltd incorporates the imprints of
Pen & Sword Archaeology, Atlas, Aviation, Battleground, Discovery,
Family History, History, Maritime, Military,
Naval, Politics, Railways, Select, Transport, True Crime, and Fiction,
Frontline Books, Leo Cooper, Praetorian Press,
Seaforth Publishing and Wharncliffe.

For a complete list of Pen & Sword titles please contact
PEN & SWORD BOOKS LIMITED
47 Church Street, Barnsley, South Yorkshire, S70 2AS, England
E-mail: enquiries@pen-and-sword.co.uk
Website: www.pen-and-sword.co.uk

Contents

Introduction

There are some wild birds who settle down in captivity. There are others who alternate between brooding on their perch and dashing themselves against the bars. Of the latter breed is Captain Hardy, once of the Connaught Rangers. Many times he dashed himself against the bars, and then at last on one glorious day he slipped between the bars and was free once more.

I can say for him what he would be the last to say for himself, that a more gallant and chivalrous gentleman never stepped. One would have thought that in the drab life of a German prison his one yearning would be for the joys of London or the peace of home. Not a bit of it. His dream of dreams was to be back in a front trench once more and at close grips with the men who had held him in bondage. So it was with many of his fellows in misfortune. When he describes how they worked at a very dangerous tunnel he adds: "Realize that they loved it and that they thought it well worth while because it *might* be the means of getting one or two men back to the war."

Like many men of action, Captain Hardy writes excellent English. Beau Brummell used to say that the really well-dressed man is the man whose dress, while absolutely adequate, calls for no attention at all. The same applies, I think, to style. A stylist is usually a writer who is affected and obscure. The man of action is clear and direct. You never observe that he has a style, but he gets his effects in a way that is clear to all, and that is the highest aim of literature. In this simple narrative, for example, one notes such little word pictures as that of the endless train of German munition waggons with giant horses and men seen in the gloom, or the picture of the Courteous

Commandant, tall, thin and pale, who gave sympathy where abuse had been expected. "Many Germans I have met," says Hardy, "whom I could respect because they were brave or because they were patriotic, but this, I think, is the only German I have ever met of whom it could be said that he was a very perfect gentleman." It is a hard saying, and many of us have been more fortunate, but certainly the writer's record justifies his remark. In England the attempted escape of an officer would always have been regarded as a sporting effort, both by civilians and officials. In Germany it was greeted with insult and execration.

Many harsh things were said by us during the war about the German treatment of prisoners. Some I said myself. With fuller information we must modify our views. The officer class was seldom ill treated when once the prison was reached. Between the place of capture and the prison, especially in the early days, the conditions were barbarous and abominable, the civilian population showing greater brutality than the military guards. The civilian camps, such as Ruhleben, were not ill managed. On the other hand, the private soldier fared well or ill according to the luck of his camp or employer. On the whole we were too much inclined to accept the occasional abominations as being universal types. Now that well-informed Germans know the treatment which their own men received in England they must feel a sense of shame at the contrast. I can recollect myself acting as sentinel over a working party of German prisoners at Lewes, and noting their ruddy rounded cheeks and well-filled jackets, at a time when our own civilian population was on a diet considerably lower than that which was given to the prisoners. Chivalry could not go further than that. The British always looked upon a war prisoner as a brave man in distress. The Germans too often regarded him as one who had deserved punishment.

Captain Hardy had fulfilment of his dream. He escaped in company with a splendid officer, with whose family I have personal ties, Captain Willie Loder-Symonds. Both men on their return at once volunteered for the front. Loder-Symonds was killed in an aeroplane smash. Hardy got back to his job, was twice wounded, got his promotion, his D.S.O. and his Military Cross with bar. The second wound involved the loss of his leg and he is now on the retired list, but a man with such inventive power and desperate energy will surely make his mark in peace as well as in war.

Arthur Conan Doyle
October 7th, 1927

Introduction to 2014 Edition

I Escape! describes numerous attempts by a young officer to escape from a variety of German prisoner of war camps, his adventures when he did break out up to his recapture and, finally, his successful 'home run' in the spring of 1918. By that stage he had been a prisoner for some three and a half years, from the time of his capture at Maroilles in late August 1914. It is an inspiring story of resolution and determination, of risk taking and initiative, of making possibilities out of seemingly nothing.

Jocelyn Lee Hardy was born in London in June 1894; his father came from County Down and his mother was a Londoner. He was commissioned in the Connaught Rangers, a few months short of his twentieth birthday, in January 1914. He was posted to the **2nd Battalion** at Aldershot, commanded by **Lieutenant Colonel A.W. Abercrombie**; and moved with it to France as part of **5 Brigade (Brigadier General R.C.B. Haking), 2nd Division (Major General C.C. Monro), I Corps (Lieutenant General Sir Douglas Haig)**. Not affected by the fighting at Mons, which was largely a II Corps battle, disaster struck the battalion on 26 and 27 August in a confused action around Le Grand Fayt, to the south east of Landrecies. Abercrombie lost control of his battalion for a variety of reasons and it became scattered. Abercrombie's group – consisting of some fifty or so men and officers, which itself was divided – was captured on 27 August in Maroilles and Hardy thus commenced his years of incarceration in Germany. What was going through Abercrombie's mind during the fateful hours of 26/27 August we shall never know, as he died as a prisoner in November

1915. The 2nd Connaughts have the unique and dubious distinction of being the only regular battalion to lose its independent identity during the war when its manpower was absorbed by the 1st Battalion in December 1914.

Hardy was faced with the rest of the conflict in a prisoner of war camp in Germany, though he had a major advantage over most other British prisoners in that he was a fluent French and German speaker. This book gives a fascinating account of how he got through his years of incarceration and describes in detail five of his escape attempts, though the Regimental history claims that he escaped nine times. The escapes were: from Augustabad, June 1915; from Halle, March 1916; from Magdeburg, June 1916; and from Fort Zorndorf, Cüstrin, where he spent his longest period as a prisoner, in the last, winter months of 1917. (There had been a very distinguished prisoner in Cüstrin many years before it was used for allied PoWs of the Great War; the future Frederick the Great was imprisoned there by his father in 1730.) Finally, Hardy was sent to Schweidnitz, from where he made his successful escape over the border into the Netherlands in March 1918.

For him the war was far from over. After an interview with the King on 18 March, he was back on the Western Front by the end of April 1918, having transferred (or, far more likely, been transferred) temporarily to the **2nd Inniskilling Fusiliers (109 Brigade, 36th (Ulster) Division)** on 22 April. On 1 August 1918 his first MC was gazetted:

Captain Jocelyn Lee Hardy, Connaught Rangers. For conspicuous gallantry and cool work in command of an offensive patrol. Proceeding about 1,000 yards in the direction of the enemy, he met a hostile party, one of whom was shot while the rest fled. At the same moment two enemy machine guns opened on his patrol at close range, one of which he promptly silenced by rapid fire. The enemy then threw a bomb, wounding him and severely wounding his sergeant. Seeing that his party would suffer heavy casualties from the machine-gun fire, he ordered them back to the lines, and remained alone with the sergeant, whom he dragged some 200 yards to a place of safety and prevented the enemy from obtaining an identification. Throughout the operation he set a splendid example to his men, and also obtained valuable information as to the enemy's dispositions.

Hardy's active war service came to an end near Dadizeele on 2 October, where his battalion was part of Second Army's breakout from the Ypres Salient. He was badly wounded in the stomach and so severely wounded in the leg that it had to be amputated (allegedly, when wounded, he shouted out, 'Stop the war! I've been hurt!'). In the series of honours' lists that followed the war, Hardy was gazetted on 30 January 1920 with a bar to his MC (which was backdated to May 1919) and a DSO. The MC was for his conduct as a PoW, his escape attempts and his ultimate success; the DSO has no specified reason for its award in the Gazette, but it is clear that his wartime service would have provided more than adequate justification. A couple of months earlier, at the beginning of November 1919, he was married; in the middle of January the following year he was on the half pay list. However, post war he was employed in the Military Intelligence Directorate in London and he continued in this employment after going on half pay.

Hardy was not one to allow a trivial matter like the loss of a leg to end his military service. He was fitted with a prosthetic leg and mastered it to the degree that he could move quite speedily and, to some degree, managed to disguise the fact that he even had one.

This did result in a rather eccentric walking style, which led to his nickname of 'Hoppy'.

He next appears in Dublin, heavily involved in the war against the IRA; he was working with the Royal Irish Constabulary, retained his Connaught Rangers' uniform and was involved in intelligence. He was mentioned in despatches in June 1920. He certainly seems to have been in the thick of things and was believed by the IRA to be involved in the shooting of Peter O'Carroll. This was followed by an incident on Saturday, 20 November 1920 in which three suspected IRA members (two were certainly senior members of the Dublin IRA) were taken into custody when found to be in possession of army uniforms and detonators. This immediately preceded the attempt by Michael Collins and the Dublin IRA to destroy the British intelligence network in a co-ordinated series of assassinations, which was only partially successful. Hardy ('Hoppy Hardy' to the IRA) was one of those targeted but it was claimed that he was away from home when the assassins came. When news of the massacres came through to Dublin Castle, and however it happened – needless to say there are conflicting accounts – the three were killed 'whilst trying to escape' and Hardy was held by the IRA to be one of those responsible. The events of the day, including the Croke Park shootings, led to it becoming known as Bloody Sunday.

At the end of that month, Hardy was put on the active list once more (again in the Connaught Rangers). He went on to survive two more serious attempts to murder him. Once in early 1921 he was tailed from Ireland to England as far as Euston Station; he seems to have been very alert or knew of the plot, because he moved very quickly into a taxi and got away. Another attempt was to be made when he returned to Dublin Docks from one of his visits; this was foiled because, by this time, he was well guarded and there was an armoured car waiting to collect him.

He was placed on the half pay list once more in November 1922; the Anglo-Irish Treaty had been signed in November 1921 and the Irish Free State formally established on 6 December 1922. In June 1922 the five regiments most closely associated with southern Ireland, including the Connaught Rangers, were disbanded. Hardy finally left the Army in spring 1925 as a result of his war wounds.

For a while Hardy worked in London for a bank – an occupation that it is a little difficult to imagine that he enjoyed. He then moved to Norfolk and went into agriculture, at Washpit Farm, which had substantial land, near King's Lynn. He also became an author of some note. His first book was the non-fictional *I Escape!* (1927), followed by a number of novels in which it is clear that the plot and some of the characters were based on his own experience. One at least went to become a play (*The Key*), based on events in the Irish Civil War, performed in the West End and was then made in a Hollywood film of the same title in 1934. This success was followed by another film, made in London in 1936, *Everything is Thunder*, with a plot based on an escaping prisoner of war.

Hardy was obviously not short of money. He owned a Rolls Royce, continued to play polo, at which he was quite successful, and undertook a round the world trip in the winter of 1936/37 with his wife and two children. It is possible that even then he had connections with British intelligence, because his tour included the militarily important ports of Yokohama and Kobe. With the outbreak of the Second World War, as a major, he commanded an anti-aircraft battery.

He wrote his last book before the war and the remainder of his life after 1945 seems to have been uneventful. He died in 1958, a relatively wealthy man (his estate was valued at some £60,000). It was said of him, in a letter to the papers after his obituary had been published, that he had 'inborn humility, a quality that often goes with great personal courage' and 'he was the easiest person to work with'. 'He had a temper that could flare easily, with a vivid sense of humour that charmed as readily as it might excite apprehension.' 'He was the friend of rich and poor, gentle and simple. His charity was profuse and secret. He loved dogs, good liquor and good company. He died as he lived – invincible.' Jocelyn Hardy is buried at Wells Church, Norfolk.

Hardy's book is well written and easy to read; he is a master story teller (and who would not be entranced by these extraordinary tales?) and a skilled wordsmith. At one level it would take only a few hours for a fast reader to finish the book; and certainly its tempo would encourage you to do that. But in the speed something would be lost, for Hardy – perhaps unsurprisingly – shows himself a keen, sensitive observer of place and of person – friend or foe; and of the emotional impact on himself of the tedium of his prison experience, the exultation in liberation and the depression of recapture. There is great detail in his description of escape plans, of the creation of escape tools, of the adaptation of unlikely objects for new purposes, of a great creative gift of adaptation, yet all achieved by the power of an understated but highly effective use of words. It is quite easy to see how Hardy went on to become an effective intelligence operator, interrogator, novelist and script writer.

In an introduction such as this only a few examples can be used to illustrate these points. In the first chapter he talks of seeing part of the advancing army passing by him: 'In the dark the limbers looked colossal – huge horses and huge men … My shame that I was no longer there to do my share consumed me. A German passed in front of me and, drawing his automatic pistol, cocked it and pointed it in my face. The escort laughed, but as for me, I thought he meant it, and I swear he could have fired it for all I cared. And that, I think, is the only time in my life I ever faced coolly the threat of death.'

His first collaborator in escaping was a Russian, Wasilief. When the latter was arrested, he attempted to shield Hardy from being taken himself. In the general confusion, 'unseen by anyone, he slipped the map and compass into my pocket, and then, turning, rejoined his captor. I have never forgotten that act of his. He longed for his freedom no less than I did, had played his part and done his share like a man right through and then, with all his hopes shattered at the last lap, turned to help me. I hope he saw the pity and distress in my eyes as we said goodbye. I hope he knew that I had done all I could to save him. Poor little man [Hardy himself was short and slim, crucial physical attributes in some of his escapes] – only twenty two, with a wife at home in Russia, and a boy he had never seen. His country has turned on him now and there is no one to welcome him home from captivity, no one to appreciate all that he has tried to do. He was the best Russian I ever met.'

He has short descriptions that yet tell so much about a man. The German commandant at Augustabad, for example, 'tall and thin and pale, totally un-German', who stood when Hardy and Wasilief entered his office after their recapture and shook hands with them. '"Gentlemen,' he said, speaking French, 'you have my sympathy. I have done all I possibly could towards your recapture, and I am astonished that your journey has lasted so long. Had I been a prisoner in England, I hope I should have acted as you have done." We were both very embarrassed and were quite at a loss for an answer.' By contrast a one liner says all one needs to know about a captive Russian general: 'This man remained comfortably seated on a form and issued constant instructions of an impossible nature.' Of those he came across in the camps, it was a Belgian, Bachwitz, whom he described as 'the best man he ever knew'. After a failed escape attempt (which involved a possible charge for murder), the two were separated and, in due course Bachwitz managed a successful escape, news Hardy first heard in a letter from home. Though he was utterly delighted for him, 'the contrast between his position and mine smote me with such a sense of depression and despair as I have seldom experienced. He was the better man, more capable, steadier; he deserved it far more than I, yet the thought of it preyed on my mind and the knowledge that I had done my last stunt with him came as a hard blow. I did not hear from him; indeed, I never heard from him until I too was a free man, but he did not need to explain to me when we met. It was a piece of understanding of which no man would have been capable who did not feel towards captivity as we two felt.'

His descriptions of the escapes, the problems in their execution, those encountered beyond the wire – how they evaded pursuers, how they fed, how they washed, how they travelled, where they slept – how all difficulties were surmounted and then the recaptures and the impact upon him: all of them are surprisingly detailed when one considers how short the book is.

Time in prison tells on him; for example, there were nine months (between June 1915 and March 1916) before he made another attempt at freedom. '… I was completely idle and the time hung very heavily on my hands. I had practically lost the power of concentrating on any book, and spent my whole day wandering round the camp but not one ray of hope could I see. Christmas came and went and March, 1916, found me in such a frantic state that I decided to discard all caution …'

And then there was the final escape. Tragically, the man who was with Hardy on the successful break out, Willie Loder-Symonds, who had been a prisoner longer than Hardy himself, was killed weeks after they got back to England. Loder was as much of an old hand at escape attempts as Hardy and proved to be an ideal companion. When they discover they are over the frontier into Holland:

'Loder was dancing in the road like a crazy creature, and I – well, I just stood there and tried to realize it. Three and a half years – three and a half years of misery and shame and bitter disappointment – three and a half years of straining after a thing longed for and that seemed as though one were never to grasp, and now one's hand closed over it and the years fell back like a dream … Oh, my readers, I wonder if any one of you have ever known such joy as I felt, sitting in the dark [by the roadside]. Were I never to know again the meaning of ease, and were I doomed forever to sorrow and catastrophe, I say that I had had more than my share of happiness in life – that nothing in life can ever stir me again as I was stirred then.'

He was twenty four years old.

Note: I would recommend that readers visit the excellent web pages on Hardy produced by David Grant, to be found at **http://www.cairogang.com/escaped/hardy/hardy.html**.

Nigel Cave, October 2014

Chapter One

It was December, 1914, and I stood idly watching a game of chemin-de-fer which was in progress in the dining-hall of Halle prisoners'-of-war camp. The hall was an appalling looking place, a disused machine room with a floor of cobbles and bricks, which was criss-crossed with trolly lines. The windows were high up and filthy, and consisted of small panes held together with iron, and the whole heavily barred. Everywhere stood dirty tables and folding-chairs, hired, I believe, from the local Biergarten, and on each table were a few rusty tins with dilapidated labels, in which the prisoners kept their food. The place was lit by a single unshaded arc-lamp high up in the roof, and its brilliance served only to enhance the squalor of the whole scene. Nothing could have been more sordid than the group which crowded round the gambling table, and it was a shock to me to realize that they were my companions, they my fellow prisoners, and that I was no more and no less than one of these. Frenchmen, Belgians, Arabs; a Cossack from the Caucasus and a Cossack of the Don, all dirty and unkempt in the extreme. An enormous Russian count held the bank. He was a civilian, captured in Germany at the outbreak of war; a huge creature with a hideously distorted face, pince-nez worn at an astonishing angle, and a crippled leg which he owed to the marksmanship of some Japanese sniper. Before him on the table lay a heap of bright tokens, for money was not allowed in the possession of prisoners. These tokens were exchangeable for goods at the canteen, but elsewhere they were valueless.

The Count was evidently having a successful bank, for a large heap of tokens lay before him on the table, and among them three twenty mark notes. Evidently some player had been reduced to parting with his carefully hoarded store of real money. I had no German money and this fact worried me, for, though my ideas were very vague on the subject, I felt I might some day find an opportunity to make a bid for liberty, and I knew that without cash I should be hopelessly handicapped. The Count looked questioningly towards me, and I betted against the whole amount, for I wanted no argument as to whom the notes belonged to. To my joy I won, and then sat down and played steadily for an hour. I lost nearly all the tokens again, but the money I kept, and that night rolled the three notes into a cigarette, for we were constantly searched.

Such small beginnings …! I used to talk sometimes about escape to the others, but one mostly got laughed at for one's pains. In those early days it was hard to find anyone who would discuss the subject seriously. The frontiers were too strongly guarded; one could not move without papers; one would be asked at once why one wasn't in uniform. A British major had attempted it the month before at Torgau, and had met his death within five miles of the camp. [This is almost certainly a reference to Major CAL Yate KOYLI, who was awarded a posthumous VC for his actions at Le Cateau on 26 August 1914. He, it is believed, committed suicide on the point of being apprehended after escaping from Torgan on 20 September 1914.] I doubt if in my heart of hearts I ever had more than golden dreams – ever had any real hope at this time. The difficulties which lay before one did indeed seem insurmountable. To break out of the camp, to cover the hundreds of miles which separated it from any frontier, and then, above all, to cross that so jealously guarded line – one dreamt of it, but even in one's dreams it was too good to be true. I was a Regular soldier, and had joined my regiment just eight months before the War. I was scarcely twenty; so early had my great chance come to me, and I had lost it. I had not even the satisfaction of feeling that my capture had been due to my having been wounded. I was a Prisoner of War and I had a whole skin. That seemed to me very dreadful, though I might well have taken comfort from the thousands of better men than myself who were in the same case. But those were days when things looked very black, not only for us prisoners but for England. I remember standing by the roadside outside a Belgian village the night after I had been taken. During the whole of that day column after column of German troops had marched past us. We had been halted by our escort to make way for an ammunition column which was passing at the trot. In the dark the limbers looked colossal – huge horses and huge men. There seemed no end to them, and my heart simply went into my mouth at the thought of our weary troops who had to face this fearful menace. My shame that I was no longer there to do my share consumed me. A German passed in front of me and, drawing his automatic pistol, cocked it and pointed it in my face. The escort laughed, but as for me, I thought he meant it, and I swear he could have fired for all I cared. And that, I think, is the only time in my life I ever faced coolly the threat of death!

Chapter Two

Of all the camps in which I have ever been, I think I can now say that Halle was the hardest camp to break. Shut in on two sides by buildings in which we lived and on the third side by the guardroom and other offices, the fourth side was defended by a barbed wire fence. Beyond this fence stood the sentries, and behind them was a high wooden fence topped with more wire. There were more sentries posted in the street outside. No one could leave the camp without passing through the guardroom, and there his papers were viséd and his photograph examined. I believe I am right in saying that, in spite of incessant efforts during a period of three years, only one man succeeded in breaking out of the camp, and he – but that is another story.

I cannot say that we were badly treated. Our lives were dreary in the extreme, however, and we lived among the grimiest surroundings. We had no recreations beyond playing cards and reading, and we worried incessantly. We got enough food in those days and our parcels were just beginning to come, but it was the sordidness of it all that overcame one. There were a certain number of civilians in the camp, for the most part old men from occupied territory. It did not seem so unfit – so indecent – that these men should be out of it all. But that we who were young, fit, trained men should be in that position – suffering no hardships and facing no dangers while thousands of half-trained men took our places at the Front – that was the grind!

For the Germans, I cannot say that they ill-treated us. In three and a half years I never saw an atrocity, though I do not, of course, know what was going on elsewhere. It may be that I hated the Germans just as much as everybody else did, and that time has soothed my feelings. It may be that the fact of their being beaten and exhausted makes one unconsciously anxious not to do them any injustice. Many lies have been told by both sides during this War, and I pray that I may not add to the number. I would rather think of the Germans as a nation labouring under a cruel regime – a nation which has been taught, as I too believe to this day, that war is a glorious thing, good for the manhood of a nation and therefore desirable; fanatical, possessed of an unaccountable hatred towards other nations; bullying and overbearing when in the ascendant, cringing before defeat, yet all the time working, working – desperately patriotic and most gallant fighting men, as we know to our cost.

For two months I walked daily round that place, but not one ray of light did I see, nor the beginning of one. The clothes of the prisoners were beginning to wear out, and the Germans, therefore, exposed dungaree trousers for sale in the canteen. They were very cheap and very flimsy, but they were civilian and I bought a pair. I had the luck to get a civilian jacket from a young Belgian officer who had lost his tunic in hospital and had been permitted to buy this one. I gave him sundry woollen waistcoats in exchange, and hid the two pieces of clothing under the floor-boards of my room, feeling, as I did so, a little easier in my mind.

It was January 1915, before the idea occurred to me that I might be able to break through the wall of the room in which I slept, into the ammunition factory on the other side. Forty of us slept in the same room, six English and the remainder French and Russians. I did not see how this plan was to be carried out without letting everybody in the room into the secret, but I decided, nevertheless, to suggest it to a young Russian who slept in a corner. We both spoke French and German, so had no difficulty in explaining ourselves, and to my joy I found him as enthusiastic on the subject as I was myself, and quite willing that work should start immediately, under his bed. He had, he told me, a friend who would work too, a man named Wasilief, who slept in a room upstairs, and whom I was destined to learn to know better. We found two huge nails in the camp and discovered that with these we could, by slow degrees, scrape out enough mortar from between the bricks to loosen them. Desperately slow work it was, and yet, careful though we were, we soon realized the impossibility of carrying on unheard at nights. We therefore chose the only alternative, to arrange that one of the party should get under the bed immediately after morning roll call and, before the others had returned to the room, to drape the blankets round the bed in such a way as to hide him, and to let him remain there until everybody had left the room for lunch.

We had laboured in this way for three days before we extracted the first brick, and this will give my readers an idea of the care we used to make no noise. Two of us sat on the bed and played cards while the third worked and, as soon as the day's task was finished, every brick had to be replaced and the whole mortared together again. To begin with we used bread for this object, but found it answered our purpose very badly indeed, and we were quite at a loss until an idea struck me. I stole from the Germans a very broad piece of plank, and cut it to fit exactly the hole which was, by then, about two feet by three. On this plank I nailed squares of wood to resemble bricks, filled the spaces with cement, and then whitewashed the whole thing. We got some lime from a Russian orderly who was in charge of such things, and this we mixed with sand, sifted through a loofah sponge, thus making a splendid cement, with which we were able to fix our dummy wall in place after each day's work.

We had removed about twenty bricks and had hidden them under the floor-boards, when the suspicions of the Germans became in some way aroused and, visiting our room one morning as we were just about to start, they pulled the beds away from the walls, and commenced to test the latter with hammers. Our work has long since been discovered and the hole filled with new bricks, but to this day one can still see the mark where that under-officer's hammer fell. It struck a real brick less than an inch above the edge of our dummy, and he passed, satisfied! Words fail me to express our delight, for we had not thought it possible that he should be deceived. We had done our work well and the fates were with us. We were fooling them; fooling them!

There were days when we could not work because the Germans were busy in the building. On these occasions we used to lie outside in the sun and, though there was no grass in the camp, and we had no view but houses all round us, we would make ourselves comfortable on a blanket and spend hours planning our journey. We had so little confidence in our ability to cross the frontier, and it lay such a great distance from us, that we decided to make for the coast, a journey of about two hundred miles, and to try to stow away on some Scandinavian ship. Generally we found we could work till about four o'clock in the afternoon, and we used then to go down to the wash room for a cold shower. I had my head cropped, for the sand caked in one's hair, and a proper young blackguard I looked! The hole under the floor-boards, where we hid the bricks, was almost full, and we were often to be seen, in the evenings, wandering about the courtyard with a suspicious bulging under our coats, for there were many rubbish heaps about the camp and we used to seize our opportunity to drop the bricks here. It is difficult to exaggerate how well or how persistently we were watched and even this little business was none too easy.

It was the end of May before we had finished with the wall, which turned out to be immensely thick. On removing the last layer of bricks we found that we were below ground level on the other side, so burrowed up, but with many forbodings, for we feared we should make a hole which would be detected by some employee in the factory. To our great satisfaction, however, we discovered that we had emerged into a disused shed which looked out upon a small courtyard, where several men were at work. The yard was surrounded by buildings, and I was not altogether surprised to see a sentry, with fixed bayonet, among the factory hands. The Germans had, as we had feared, anticipated just such an attempt as we had made, but this did not, of course, mean that we were beaten yet. I ran little risk of being seen where I stood for, though there was no front wall to the shed, those outside stood in bright sunlight while I was in deepest shadow. I therefore waited until the hooter sounded to cease work, and watched the men leave and pass round an angle formed by a building. Where they went to, once out of my sight, I had, of course, no means of knowing, but I thought it probable they were obliged to pass through a wicket and hand in their checks to a watchman. Whether there were any other means of exit remained to be seen.

I crawled back and we closed up for the day, but I would not talk until we had put everything straight, and had swept the floor. When this was done we lit cigarettes and sat down on the bed, and after I had told them everything I had seen we decided that I should have to make a reconnaissance that night. It would, as a matter of fact, suit us very much better to break out during the night, for there was no roll call between 10 p.m. and 9 a.m., whereas there were three during the day.

I went to bed at the usual time, but was up soon after midnight, and crawled along to our corner, where I found that the Russian had prepared everything for me. I got straight through, but was careful to make no noise, knowing that the sentry might be standing just at the opening of the shed. I had no sooner got to the front of this little building than the sentry passed within a yard of me, and I had scarcely time to shrink back, being obliged to stand absolutely motionless, till he turned and walked some distance from me. The whole courtyard upon which I looked was brilliantly lighted by an arc-lamp in the centre, and also by the lamps placed at intervals along the roof of the building in which we lived. I remained stationary here for some time, but the only two pieces of information which I gained were that work ceased at about 1.30 a.m. and that a night watchman was on duty, in addition to the sentry. This complicated matters badly, though God knows what I had expected to find. I crept back, and set about replacing the board, which I found no easy task in the dark – but I did not dare to leave it till the morning, for many of the Russian orderlies who swept the rooms were not to be trusted and it was literally as important to hide what we had done from them as from the Germans.

The next morning we held a council of war, and decided to ask a certain Frenchman, who lived in our room, whether he would care to join us in the affair. This man was the picture of a German, and he had a German name. The point about him, however, which concerned us was that he spoke most perfect Boche, spoke it better, in fact, than he did French. Our idea was that, with this man to act as spokesman, we might be able to lull the suspicions of the sentry should we find it necessary to pass him. It will be seen by this that I had no great confidence in my German accent at that time, though the day was to come when I could converse without any anxiety. We spoke to the Frenchman that afternoon, and having heard the full details, he said that he was prepared to do his part. He was, we found, a stern, silent man, and since my experience with him I have had a horror of the order. Most of them appear at a pinch to be worse than useless, and he was no exception. However, we were very young and inexperienced, and delighted at having such a man to help us. We arranged that the break out should take place two nights later, and our excitement during those forty-eight hours can well be imagined. We all found that we had no appetite for our food, could not sit still for two minutes on end, but spent the whole time wandering round the camp, smoking cigarettes and feeling intensely mysterious.

At last *the* night came. Evening roll call was over and the Germans had left our room. We started at once to get into our civilian clothes, and I remember the looks of astonishment on the faces of the other prisoners. They realized, however, that somehow or other we intended "going over the top", and many of them came up and shook hands, wishing us luck. We were very nervous of course, but it was impossible to help laughing as we looked at each other's shabby get-up. One of the Russians was, I noticed, fairly drunk. This had been his way of making sure of himself! I was furious and cursed him in three or four languages, but he merely grinned sheepishly and sat down rather suddenly on his bed. There was nothing to be done about it, so I got under the bed and crawled straight through, followed by the Frenchman. Behind him came Wasilief, but the other Russian never got beyond the hole, where he lay and eventually fell asleep! The Frenchman whispered to me to crawl out and see if there was any outlet to the left. This was no pleasant task, but I supposed it had to be done, so, taking advantage of a long black shadow across the yard. I moved out on my stomach until I had a clear view. Neither to left nor right was there any exit, while in front of me was the corner round which I had seen the workmen disappear. This then was the only way.

Suddenly the sentry turned and started to walk towards me. My first inclination was to get up and run into the shed, and it was only with the greatest effort that I restrained myself though I knew it would be fatal. I began to crawl back as quickly as I possibly could, but with my heart in my mouth, for I did not see how he could fail to detect me. It was only by a miracle that he did so fail, and I stood shaking in the shed as he passed. As soon as I had recovered from my horribly narrow escape I explained to the Frenchman that we must walk boldly across the yard, and trust to his knowledge of German should we be challenged, and I asked him if he was ready. To my utter astonishment he replied that he would not dream of doing as I suggested! I had misrepresented the whole affair to him and he was not going to make a fool of himself. I tried every argument, but in vain; Wasilief then spoke to him in Russian. I do not know much Russian myself, but I understood my plucky little slit-eyed friend that time, and I do not think that the most drunken British navvy could have competed against him. But it left old red-beard cold, so there was nothing to do but abandon the project, for without him we were helpless. I went back first, and, finding the other Russian asleep in the tunnel, derived a certain amount of satisfaction from stamping on his face, which he had incautiously left exposed at the opening. He finally woke up, bleary-eyed and muddled, and started to back out. I kicked out steadily until I was through into the room, and then, without waiting for the others, undressed and got into bed. At five o'clock I was up again, replaced the board and mortared it in. We did not sleep much, for we had made a bad mess of it. I had discovered two cowards, and the only man worth anything was Wasilief. We would be the laughing-stock of the whole camp, and everybody would know in a few days. We had got to act quickly, we had got to leave the Frenchman out, and we had got to prevent the other Russian coming if we possibly could. All these things were plain, and I decided I would make a reconnaissance during the lunch hour that day.

Accordingly the moment the room was empty at midday I fairly leapt into my civilian clothes, crawled through the hole, and, getting up, walked openly across the courtyard and round the corner beyond which we had not been able to see. The sentry glanced at me, but I grinned back and he said nothing. The moment I turned the corner I was confronted by two high wooden doors under which ran a railway track. They were shut, and beside them stood a small office, though whether it was at that moment occupied I could not see. I returned, and to my relief saw that the sentry had walked to the end of his beat and would not therefore see me enter the shed. In another minute I was back in my room full of what I had seen, only to be greeted with a blank stare by Wasilief, and to be told by him that he and I, with about eighty other officers, were to be sent to another camp, and that we were leaving that same night.

My heavens! what a blow it was. For one moment we wondered, would it be possible to try at once, but a glance at our watches showed us the futility of the idea. Within five minutes the factory hands would be back at work, and it would take us twice as long as that to assemble our things. No, we were done, and all that was left to us was to make the best of any new chances that might come our way. For two things we had to be grateful – we were going together, and our new camp was only fifty miles from the Baltic coast. It *was* a new camp and probably not as strongly guarded as it would be later.

We were to have our baggage ready for examination at six o'clock in the evening, and knew that we should be personally searched. We therefore arranged with some officers to hand us our *verbotene* things after we had been searched and had fallen in with the party. All this went off smoothly and at nine o'clock that night we marched out of the camp. I felt very mortified over what had passed, and very worried. Many of my companions knew by now what I had been attempting. People have not much sympathy with a man who fails, and I thought I saw sly winks, which distressed me immensely. Youth certainly has its disadvantages!

Chapter Three

As soon as we arrived at Augustabad I saw that we had a very easy proposition in front of us. Many camps were, I believe, fairly easy to break out from in those comparatively early days of the War, but against this must be remembered the total lack of experience on our part. We had nothing to go upon, did not know what actions were likely to draw suspicion on us, once out of the camp; and there were practically none of us who could depend upon our knowledge of German to pull us through. We did not even know the status of an escaped prisoner of war recaptured in civilian clothes, but the general impression was that he could be shot as a spy. Far be it from me to disparage the efforts of those who came later, for many of them made wonderful attempts and showed the most admirable skill and courage; but they learned much from our failures. They arrived in camps where escape was a general topic of conversation and, from almost their first day of captivity, heard stories and advice on the subject – became, in fact, familiar with the idea. In the days I write of now, one felt rather a lone wolf, was regarded doubtfully by most people, and one had to think and shift for oneself.

It is a peculiar fact, and perhaps worth recording, that I felt my captivity very much more at Augustabad than in any place where I have since been. The camp was a hotel which had been converted, and the food, though not too plentiful, was good, while the staff were polite and our rooms clean and comfortable. My first idea was to apply to be transferred to some other camp, and allow a wounded man to take my place but, on thinking the matter over,

I realized that I would be foolish so to throw away my chances of getting home. I was only in the camp for ten days, but was perfectly miserable during the whole of that time, and I do not think I was hypersensitive in that it seemed to me abominable that I should be leading a life of comfort at such a time. It was never again my lot to find myself in a good camp; and of that I am glad. I should hate to think that pleasant surroundings would have been deterrent to me in my efforts to get away, but that they did have weight with many people is a fact beyond dispute.

There were so many possibilities about Augustabad that it frightened us, for it seems very much worse to fail over an easy stunt than over an ordinary one. It was several days before we had decided on our method, and what we eventually did was so simple that I am almost ashamed to make a chapter of it. Still, it is all a part of the story and, incidentally, marks the end of ease for me, for I never had another easy one, but went to the job each time with the prospect of a bullet in my back.

Practically every day there was a bathing parade, for which we fell in and were marched out of the camp and down to the lake under guard. Sentries were posted and every precaution was taken to see that no one slipped away. There was even an armed sentry in a boat among the bathers. But apparently the impossibility of anyone hiding and remaining there when the party was marched away had not occurred to the under-officer in charge. He used to make a show of counting us, but it did not appear to me that he considered this more than a necessary formality, for he was obviously careless about it. Wasilief and I, having noticed this, carried down our civilian clothes wrapped in towels and hid them among the bushes. With mine I put two packets of chocolate, a small tin of malted milk and my compass, with a small-scale map of Northern Germany which I had found. The following day was wet and we had resigned ourselves to waiting, when suddenly at the last moment it was announced that the bathing parade "in spite of the rain place take would," which is the simple way in which the German explains himself. I ran off and got Wasilief, thinking that it would be as well to go down, if only to make sure that our kits had not been touched. As we marched down I noticed two French officers carrying large bundles, precisely as we had done the day before. I asked one of them what he had in his bundle, and he said that he was taking down clothes to wash. I knew well that this was a lie, and the moment we fell out I rushed up to Wasilief and told him we were going to be jumped and that, although we had not enough food, our only hope was to go that afternoon. He agreed at once and we promptly hid in the bushes.

The moment we were there I know I for one regretted it. It was impossible that the Germans would be idiotic enough to let us slip through their fingers so easily. The moment the party fell in to march away our absence would be noticed and there would be the devil of a scene; the bushes would be searched and we should be found and brought out like a pair of fools. We could not possibly rejoin the others now, for the sentries were in position and would see us come out of our hiding place. So there we lay. We could see the bathers from where we were, and we were able to watch the under-officer as he stood on the bank. Apparently he had not noticed that we were not in the water, for he remained quite unperturbed, and after about fifteen minutes gave the order to start dressing. Another few minutes and the party fell in within a few yards of us. The last man came out of the bathing-hut, drying his hair as he came. The German looked into the hut and then closed and locked the door and walked back to the party. He would count them, I thought; pause, count them again; shout out that some were missing! The sentries would run towards him, adjusting their safety catches as they ran. All would be lost.

"March," said he and, scarcely able to believe my eyes, I saw the escort fall in on the flanks and rear as the party disappeared among the trees. We stared at each other. Were we dreaming or had we really done it? Oh, how wonderful it felt – that first time! Our whole outlook on life was changed. It did not seem possible that they could get us again now. We laughed as we tore off our uniforms and hid them in the sand, and jeered at the Germans as we pulled on our awful "civvies". Why, it had been ridiculously easy – just a little cheek, that was all one needed!

We had seen nothing of the Frenchmen and were not specially anxious to. We started off through the woods and made a huge detour round the town of Neu-Brandenburg, which lay to the north of the camp. It was pretty hard going – very undulating ground and great masses of the previous autumn's leaves to wade through. After about two hours we were clear of the woods and came into flat open country. Here we were held up for some time by a stream over which we could find no bridge. Eventually we decided to swim it, and this we did, first tying our things up in bundles and throwing them over. This stream turned out to be about seven feet deep – two feet of water and five of mud. We were black when we got out on the other side, and very little could we do to improve our appearance, for we had no towels. However, we had no time to waste and couldn't let a little mud delay us.

We had intended to keep to open country, but the road looked so very inviting that we moved down on to it, and had gone about four miles when suddenly we stopped with one accord. About fifty yards ahead, in front of a small inn, stood a sentry looking towards us with his rifle slung, and holding a large dog on a leash. I pulled out my watch and, remarking in German that it was time we got back, turned and walked towards the town with Wasilief beside me. I glanced back and noticed to my horror that the sentry was following us. One side of the road was wired, on the other lay a flat and open field. We redoubled our pace and heard our pursuer break into a run. Then we let ourselves go. Never in my life have I bolted so madly as I bolted then. Behind me I heard whistle blasts and then the cry of the sentry, "Halt! sonst schiesse ich" ("Halt! or I fire"). A road ran up to the left, leading to a farm; it was wired on both sides, but it was our only hope, for our further retreat towards Neu-Brandenburg was now cut off by a cart full of harvesters, which had pulled up when the driver saw us coming. Up this little road we dashed, and as we drew near to the farm a tremendous barking of dogs broke out and people came out of the buildings to see what the trouble was. Whether or not they tried to stop us, I do not know. The fact remains that we were much too frightened and going much too fast to *be* stopped! We went through that farmyard with a grand rush – round to the left – over a gate – through a field and then over some wire, where the best part of my dungarees went west; then through a plantation of young firs and across more fields – on and on until we fell exhausted.

For at least five minutes we lay there panting and helpless on the ground. Mein Gott! If we were going to have to do this sort of thing often, the sooner it was all over the better! We sat up and looked at each other drearily. All sounds of pursuit had ceased; evidently the sentry had not released his dog, probably because it was only half-trained, and I do not doubt that his efforts to hold it in had prevented his firing. We were indeed well out of it, but we had been badly shaken and were not going to take any more chances if we could help it. We thought it possible that the Germans were organizing some sort of pursuit and if this was the case we must not waste a moment; so we got up and, having located ourselves roughly on the map, set off again. I think we scarcely stopped once during the next six hours, except to drink out of puddles and to light the single pipe which we had between us. We went round all villages and kept off roads. The country looked wonderfully beautiful in the moonlight. Great expanses of standing corn, picturesque little villages built round their square-towered churches – all very peaceful and seeming very far removed from the War and – for the German peasant goes early to bed – over all a great silence.

Day was just breaking when we stopped. Near us lay a small copse where we thought we might rest during the day. We got in among the underbrush and lay down, but it was impossible to sleep, for we were soaked with dew and very cold, and the mosquitoes were appalling. These things, combined with the fact that we had eaten more than half our chocolate, induced us to push on after a very miserable two hours. Several people were by now at work in the fields and some of them looked at us curiously; one man, I remember, spoke to us but appeared quite satisfied with my answers. It was very hot that day and we were reduced to drinking out of the dirtiest little pools. About midday we were delayed for nearly two hours crossing a river about a hundred and twenty yards wide, the only bridge anywhere near us being right in the centre of a very large village. We didn't dare chance this, so we had to swim for it with our clothes on our heads. If I remember correctly, I had to cross four times, making eight journeys, for Wasilief, like most Russians, was a poor swimmer, though God knows he would have tried to swim the Channel had it been necessary, for he had all the pluck in the world.

Just as I had crossed for the last time a man rode down to within twenty yards of us, scrutinized us most carefully and then, turning his horse, rode away. It was evident that our descriptions were out, and we had to dress at top speed and take to our heels again. We covered about another ten miles, had a splendid meal of green peas which we found growing in a field, and then burrowed down into a haystack and fell asleep with a delightful sense of warmth and security. It was about nine o'clock in the evening when we awoke. We were both desperately stiff and blistered, bleary-eyed and tousled, and covered with various insect-bites. At first we could scarcely walk, but our joints soon loosened and before long we were making fine progress again. We were beginning to get a little bolder, and indeed we could no longer afford to make many detours, for we had no food left and very little tobacco. That night we kept to the roads, despite all our other resolutions, and passed through many silent little villages, on such sandy lanes that one could hardly hear one's own foot-falls, and scarcely a dog barked.

It was dawn before we reached the outskirts of Greifswald, a fairly large town built on an inlet, and we walked through the silent streets, glancing uneasily at the police station as we passed it, and then halted on the bank of a canal, where we sat and smoked the last of our tobacco. It was a most beautiful morning and, in the bright sunshine, we looked even more dilapidated than I had imagined. We were dirty, our hands and faces were covered with scratches, our eyes were bloodshot, and we badly needed a shave. I took off my trousers and tied up the rents as best I could with a piece of my bootlace, and we washed our faces, using grit, for we had no soap. I remember how we cursed those Frenchmen who had forced us to leave at such short notice and so ill-prepared, and we wondered what their fate had been.

By seven o'clock we judged that the shops must be opening, so tramped back into the town, where, with much trepidation, we entered a butcher's shop and bought a pound of coarse sausage. It contained large pieces of skin with hair still on them, but this did not deter us from making a meal of it. In another shop we bought some cheese, and were also able to buy cigarettes, but bread, of course, we had to go without, for we were limited to what was coupon-free. There did not appear to be many ships in Greifswald harbour and, our objective being Stralsund, we set off north again.

We were both very fagged by now, and we quarrelled incessantly during the whole of that day. It must be remembered that we had the greatest difficulty in explaining anything but the simplest ideas to each other, for Wasilief spoke only a very few words of French and German, while one or two phrases in Russian were all that I knew of his tongue. Beyond this, we used signs! About midday, we most rashly stopped outside a small roadside inn and ordered some beer. We sat drinking it at a table, and when people passed us I muttered in German to my companion. We had finished our beer and were just about to go, when a man shouted to us from the door of the inn, and, on turning, I saw that he was pointing to something which lay under the table. It was the envelope in which Wasilief always carried the photograph of his wife, and, along the top, were stamped the words in large print: "Kriegsgefangenen Sendung!" ("Prisoners of War post!") By a huge stroke of luck the man had evidently not noticed this, so I picked up the envelope and handed it back to my friend; but I wish to Heaven I had destroyed it, for it was destined to stand me in bad stead.

We covered a lot of ground that afternoon and evening, but we had to stop very often now, for we were getting rather done. By sunset we were within ten miles of Stralsund and had the good fortune to find another large haystack. It was unpleasantly near a village, but we saw no other, so, climbing up to the top by means of a ladder, we made ourselves comfortable, and no one on earth slept better than we did that night.

We were off again by six the following morning, but spent a long time trying to pick some wild cherries off a tree, of which we got about fifty and considered ourselves well paid for our trouble. Stralsund was in sight when we passed a small creek. The water looked so inviting and we were so hot that we left the road and, walking down to the sandy beach, undressed and swam out. The water was perfect, but our pleasure was cut short by the arrival of several German soldiers with their towels on the same errand. They spoke to us once or twice, and I was at great pains to hide my tattoo marks, which I feared would be included in my official description. It was with great relief that we left these fellows behind us and entered Stralsund.

Never again in my life shall I see an English seaside town on a bright summer morning without my thoughts carrying me back to that day in Stralsund in July, 1915. The white sunlit streets and the black shadows thrown by the awnings of the shops; everywhere convalescent officers and flappers; soldiers of course by the hundred, and a general air of cheerfulness and well-being over all. It is a wonderful thing how sights and smells and sounds carry one back to earlier times in one's life. I remember once at the Front, not many months before the end, finding myself in a captured German dug-out. Around me lay pieces of German equipment, on a shelf were several loaves of black bread, and everywhere hung the all-pervading smell of the Boche. I was prepared for a curious revival of past sensation when I cut a piece of the bread and began to eat it while I glanced at the leading article of a two days' old *Tägliche Rundschau*; but I could not have believed that the illusion would be so extraordinarily vivid … I was back in Germany, a prisoner again. I was in a guardroom, just recaptured on an escape stunt … If half a dozen Landsturm men had come in through the doorway of the dug-out, I do not think I should have been in the slightest surprised or concerned!

On the quay we bought a lot of cherries from an old woman. These we finished in no time, and Wasilief went off and bought some strawberries, after having made quite sure of the German equivalent. There were many ships in harbour and presently, leaving Wasilief to sleep in the shadow of a goods truck, I went off to examine them.

Chapter Four

I felt that, looking, as I did, more or less like a farm labourer, I was rather out of place in the harbour, so took off my coat and boots and set out along the quay. The majority of the ships in port appeared to be nothing more than fishing smacks, and these did not, of course, interest me. Certain ships were taking their cargoes on board, but in every such case there were German officials on deck. At last I heard two men, on a small schooner, talking what I judged to be Swedish, so went on board and, taking one of the men aside, offered him a twenty-mark note, and said in German: "You can have this if you'll tell me how I can get back to Sweden."

He did not take the note at once, but replied:

"Why, you can get a ticket from the steamship company."

"Yes," I said, "but what if one has no papers?"

"Oh, that's different. How old are you?" he asked with a grin, evidently thinking I was a German who wished to evade military service.

"I'm nineteen," I answered, "and I'll give two thousand marks to anybody who lands me at the American Consulate in Trelleborg (Sweden). It's not what you think it is. I've got plenty of money and I swear you'll be paid if you help me."

He looked at me curiously for a moment and then, walking over to his companion, whispered with him for some time. I could not hear a word of what was being said, and feared, as he came back towards me, that I should merely be ordered off the ship. Instead he muttered to me, in a low voice:

"This ship sails tonight for Sweden!"

Never in my life have I known such exultation as I felt then. It was finished; in twenty four hours I should be a free man, and within a few days I should be home. I dared not show my delight, but called up the cabin-boy and, giving him another twenty mark note, sent him off to fetch some beer. The more familiar I appeared to be with the crew, the less chance was there of my being detected, and I wanted to make sure of their being in good humour before I mentioned to them the fact that I had a companion. The beer arrived, and I refused any change from the boy, for I thought it important to make an impression on the men. One of them lifted his bottle.

"Na, Prosit!" said he, and as he spoke a shadow fell across the deck, and a raucous, guttural voice cried: "Eh! I say! you spick Englis – ain't it?" I looked up, and there on the edge of the quay stood a burly civilian, holding Wasilief tightly by the arm, and my heart sank within me, for I knew that the worst had happened. We were done – done; but I wasn't going to give up without a struggle, so I looked up innocently and replied: "Ah spick him a leedle bit, y'know." "Veil," said the civilian, shaking Wasilief, "vot's dat for a man, eh? He say you know him. He says he's been a Norwegian, and I know five language and I try him Norwegian, and he vasn't answer not von plooty vord. Den I try him Englis, and he tell me you unterstand Englis. Dat's a Rooshian, *I* say." He turned to Wasilief and, holding out a metal disc which proved him to be a member of the harbour police, continued to yell and howl at him in various languages. Poor little Wasilief looked helplessly at me, and then I started, very carefully, and in very broken English, to say that I had met him the day before, that we had got drunk together, and that, in consequence, his ship had left without him. His papers, I said, he had left on board. His father, I believed, was a Pole, who had become naturalized as a Norwegian. Never for an instant did it occur to the German that I was using my mother tongue. He obviously thought that we were merely employing English as a mutual language and it gave him great satisfaction to air his knowledge in front of the little crowd which had formed. Nothing, however, that I could say was of the slightest avail, and I had to watch my poor little friend dragged off very forcibly. For a moment he wrenched himself free, and, running back, jumped down on the deck again, at which manoeuvre the shouts of the policemen became terrifying. But, undismayed, Wasilief walked across to me and said goodbye, while at the same time, unseen by anyone, he slipped the map and compass into my pocket, and then, turning, rejoined his captor.

I have never forgotten that act of his. He longed for his freedom no less than I did, had played his part and done his share like a man right through, and then, with all his hopes shattered at the last lap, turned to help me. I hope he saw the pity and distress in my eyes as we said goodbye. I hope he knew that I had done all I could to save him. Poor little man – only twenty two, with a wife at home in Russia, and a boy he had never seen. His country has turned on him now, and there is no one to welcome him home from captivity, no one to appreciate all he has tried to do. He was the best Russian I ever met.

The fact of Wasilief's capture, bitterly though I regretted it, certainly simplified matters for me. Evidently unsuspected, with only five hours to go; Germany behind me, and in front of me the open sea, I felt almost secure. Indeed, so convinced was I of success, that my thoughts were chiefly concerned with the best method of helping other prisoners and conveying news to them. I saw myself as a sort of Scarlet Pimpernel – the hero of a hundred escapes! After all, I had talked with a detective – talked English – that was the incredible thing. If that were possible, surely I was justified in thinking that the fates were with me.

Deeming it as well to appear busy, I picked up a bucket which lay on the deck, and was going ashore to fetch some water, when I stopped. Running at full speed along the quay side towards me, came the policeman, with another man in uniform. He was bawling at the top of his voice:

"Where is he? Where is he? That man's a British officer."

There were many people on the quay, and my only way of escape lay overboard, and to jump would, of course, have been worse than useless. So I stood there and waited, with the bottom fallen out of my life. The German uttered a yell of excitement when he saw me, and, rushing on board, seized me by the wrist, shouting to every one in general: "I've got him, I've got him!" and appearing as triumphant as though he had been pursuing me for months. He pulled a slip of paper out of his pocket, and, glancing at it, said:

"You are the English Lieutenant Hardy, escaped from Augustabad. I arrest you in the name of the law."

His companion produced a small automatic, and went through the usual formula, but it was quite unnecessary, now that they had searched me and taken my map and compass. I was quite helpless, and had no choice but to go quietly with them. A terrific harangue was delivered to the sailors for allowing me on board without first demanding my papers, and I was then led off through the town. This was a horrible experience, for there were many officers and pretty girls about, and everybody stared at me. I felt my position most keenly, for I was not so hardened in those days as I grew perforce to be.

As I walked between them towards the police station, they told me that Wasilief had refused to say what or who he was, but that they had detected him trying to get rid of that tell-tale envelope. They had taken it from him and had, of course, immediately identified him as the escaped Russian. They had, they said, been on the look out for some time, but had never conceived it possible that officers of any nationality would so demean themselves as to dress as beggars! Wasilief told me afterwards that, the moment they had discovered what he was, the policeman had stopped for an instant with his mouth open, and had then cried:

"Aber, mein Gott, der mann spricht Englisch, wie ich Deutsch!" ("But, my heavens, the man speaks English like I do German.")

Without another word he had rushed out of the office and called to a companion, and the two had then seized their bicycles, and ridden down again to the harbour at full speed.

I cannot say that they were altogether bad fellows, and they seemed to entertain a certain amount of respect towards us for what we had done. Of course it was foolish, because no one could escape from Germany. But then – all Englishmen were fools, and it was partly on account of that that England was going to be destroyed. Few Germans omitted this fact when talking to prisoners.

I was taken into the police station, searched and then locked up in a cell. My braces were taken from me to prevent my hanging myself but, though very depressed, I do not think that I should have gone to those lengths. My feelings at that time are hard to analyse, for I was fearfully disappointed, but not so cast down or hopeless as one would imagine. I had tried and done my best, and from now on I knew that I should never rest until I was a free man. I had failed where many others might have succeeded, but the fact remains that they had not cared to try; I felt I was beginning to justify my existence again, and the germ of hope was born in me.

The following day the escort arrived to take us back to Augustabad. They appeared very hostile towards us, and the under-officer in charge, who had a most bullying manner, forbade Wasilief and me to speak to each other. Much to our astonishment, one of the escort suddenly asked him, during the journey, why he could not treat us properly, and added that were he a prisoner he too would try to escape. This remark was merely greeted with a furious gesture, but there was some slight change in his manner towards us. We heard that the Frenchmen had been retaken almost immediately.

On arriving at the camp we were marched straight to the Commandant's office. I had expected to be greeted with abuse and insults, to both of which we were well accustomed, but this man's treatment of us was almost unnerving. I can see him now – tall and thin and pale, totally un-German – rising from his seat as we came in and offering his hand.

"Gentlemen," he said in French, "you have my sympathy. I have done all I possibly could towards your recapture, and I am astonished that your journey has lasted so long. Had I been a prisoner in England, I hope I should have acted as you have done."

We were both very embarrassed and were quite at a loss for an answer. Many Germans I have met whom I could respect because they were brave, or because they were patriotic, but this, I think, is the only German I have *ever* met of whom it could be said that he was a very perfect gentleman.

We were not, of course, allowed back in the camp, nor were we permitted to have any intercourse with the other prisoners. We were each locked up in a separate room of the building in which the guardroom was situated, but beyond lack of exercise, suffered no hardships or privations. We were visited one day by the general in command of the group of camps to which Augustabad belonged, and he appeared far from friendly, but on hearing that my regiment was the Connaught Rangers, he became much impressed, and said:

"Connaught – Connaught – *Duke* of Connaught! Him have I met in your Aldershot!"

After this he was very much more civil, and told me that I should be sent to another camp after three weeks. He did not mention that the camp to which I was to be transferred was Halle, and it was a sad day for me when I got the news. I had no hope whatever that our tunnel would be still available, for it had become public property, and was certain to have been discovered by now. It was a cruel blow to me, and dashed all my new-born hopes to the ground, but I had to face it as best I could, and comfort myself with the thought that I went back to Halle a better man than I had left it.

Our uniforms had been dug up and given back to us, and our civilian clothes had, of course, been confiscated. We were told that they would be sent to the orderly room of our new camp, and handed back to us at the end of the War. Well, I didn't wait for mine!

Chapter Five

I mmediately upon arriving at Halle I was, for no reason which I have ever yet discovered, sent to prison again for four days. This was, however, no great hardship, and incidentally gave me the opportunity of regaining my civilian clothes, for I picked them up without being seen while passing through the orderly room. This was a great piece of luck and cheered me up somewhat. Our fellow prisoners showed the greatest interest in the account of our adventures and several of them mentioned to me that, should I have any further plans, they would do all in their power to help me. Beyond the fact that the tunnel had, as I expected, been discovered, and that rather more wire had been added at certain points, the camp was little changed. About twenty new officers, taken in the Second Battle of Ypres [21 April–25 May], had arrived, and some of them, though much younger than myself, had been three and four months at the Front. I used to listen to their accounts of the fighting with the greatest envy and inward chagrin, for I thought incessantly of the Front, imagining myself in the thick of it again, and such names as Ypres and Arras came to hold for me an indescribable romance. A Frenchman who had been present when the tunnel was discovered told me the details of the affair. It appeared that a sentry in the factory had noticed to his astonishment that the voices of prisoners talking in the room were plainly audible on his side of the wall. He had reported this fact and the Germans had made a search in the room, but had found nothing to raise their suspicions. An examination had then been made on the factory side of the wall, and, on the opening of the tunnel being discovered, a long iron bar was pushed through and our poor dummy fell into the room. The Commandant, I was told, was furious and a young German officer who remarked that it was a wonderful piece of work got badly told off for his pains. Nothing could of course be proved, but I found myself suspect, and was ordered to take up my abode in the dining-hall, where place had been made for about one hundred beds. This building I have already tried to describe. We slept on the first floor, and the ground floor was constantly visited by the rounds; it was kept light all night, and, as the sentries had a clear view of the interior through the windows, any possibility of tunnelling was out of the question. From this place there was nothing whatever to be done. Various schemes were on foot in the camp, and on the strength of such experience as I had had I was generally invited to take a hand in these affairs. But, one after another, plans fell through, and I began to realize that escape from Halle was very nearly an impossibility.

I kept myself always "mobilized", as we called it, that is to say, I always had by me a small untouched store of food, a compass which I had managed to buy from a British orderly, and my civilian clothes, which I had packed into a tin and buried in the dining-hall. One night in November, Wasilief tiptoed into my room at about eleven o'clock and, waking me, whispered in my ear. What he told me brought me out of bed in an instant, and I dragged on my clothes and followed him out of the room. He led me down into the hall where a small group of Russians were talking in excited whispers..

It appeared that they had made a key for the door which led from the dining-hall into the kitchen, which room was not visited by the Germans during the night. By breaking through the back wall of the kitchen they would, they believed, emerge into a small courtyard from which they could reach the street. German cooks were employed and it was therefore thought necessary that the work should be finished in one night, for it would certainly be noticed in the morning. The Russians went on the assumption that if they made sufficient noise the Germans would never attribute it to prisoners, but would take it for granted that their own workmen were busy fitting a new oven or something of the kind and that they had been obliged to take advantage of the only time when the kitchen was free. I had been told by an orderly that a sentry was posted in the little courtyard, but nevertheless neither Wasilief nor myself intended to lose the smallest chance. By the tremendous din which issued from the kitchen we knew that work had already started, so we volunteered to relieve those already at work in half an hour. We hurried off and unearthed our civilian clothes, got dressed, filling our pockets with the things we hoped to need, and then rejoined the others in the hall. The party consisted, so far as I remember, of seven Russians, one of whom was a general, who by virtue of his rank was not expected to work. This man remained comfortably seated on a form and issued constant instructions of an impossible nature.

On being led into the kitchen the first thought that crossed my mind was that there had been an air-raid! It was extraordinary the amount of damage that those fellows had been able to do in such a short time. In order the better to get at the wall they had completely demolished a large brick stove and the debris from it lay all over the floor. Two Russians, stripped to the waist, were attacking the wall like maniacs, while a third knelt at the window watching one of the sentries whose beat took him past the building. The room was dimly illumined by the light in the courtyard of the camp, but it would have been almost impossible for the sentry to have seen what was going on, even had he pressed his face against the window. Wasilief and I did about an hour's work, and being the only Britisher in the affair I felt it incumbent on me to make a good show, and worked myself almost to a standstill. By about 2 a.m. the wall had been pierced and I, being the smallest member of the party, slipped off my boots and wriggled through. I found myself in a large garage and quickly satisfied myself that there was no means of exit, except by the large doors at the end. These were locked, but the upper halves were fitted with panes of glass and looked out on a very small courtyard. Beyond this yard was the open street, and for a moment I thought we were free men. But suddenly something moved and a sentry stepped out of the shadows into full view. I ducked and crept back. There was much consternation when I made my report, though Wasilief and myself had scarcely dared to hope for anything better, and I was at once taken off to the General. I told him there was a sentry stationed in the courtyard.

"Kill him," said the General, and made a sweeping gesture with his hand.

"But who's going to—?"

"Kill him," he repeated, and sat back with the resigned air of one accustomed to dealing with idiots.

Each man in turn investigated the garage to satisfy himself that my information was correct; and then one and all agreed that they could get no further and must now take the necessary steps to avert suspicion themselves. They accordingly smothered the place with pepper, that no trace of scent might betray them to the police dogs, and dusted their clothes with it as thoroughly as possible. The General continued to reiterate that they should have *killed* the sentry, but no one took any notice of him. I had finished cleaning my clothes, so I took them along and hid them again and then ran upstairs, which was most unwise on my part, for the Russians, hearing me running, thought that the Germans had arrived on the scene and stampeded. They shouted, threw their things right and left, and dashed past me up the stairs, for I had paused to see what all the trouble was about. When I reached my bed I found some one crouching under it. It was the General! In one hand he held a short iron bar, with the other he grasped a bottle of brandy by the neck! Then I understood. Needless to say, all this noise finally brought the Germans with dogs and lanterns, but the pepper had done its work and not one of the culprits was ever identified.

From this time on I was completely idle and the time hung very heavily on my hands. I had practically lost the power of concentrating on any book, and spent my whole day wandering round the camp, but not one ray of hope could I see. Christmas came and went, and March, 1916, found me in such a frantic state that I decided to discard all caution and attempt a stunt which I had been vaguely considering for some time.

On three sides the camp was, as I have said, shut in by buildings. Those on two sides were occupied by the prisoners, the third was a long two-storied building, and contained the guardroom, the parcel room, and upstairs the German quartermaster's store. This building was not accessible to the prisoners except during the time that parcels were being given out. In front of it ran a high barbed wire fence with a gate in the centre, at which a sentry was stationed. When one went to get parcels the sentry allowed one to pass through the fence and walk to the parcel room, from which there was no other exit. To get there one walked down a short passage; half way down the latter was a staircase which led up to a landing, on which were two doors, one that of the censor's office, the other that of the quartermaster's stores. This latter was invariably locked.

Now beyond this building was a very small garden where a sentry was stationed; it was lit at night by a bright arc-lamp and was cut off from the street by high iron railings. I am afraid that all this is very difficult to follow, but I may perhaps simplify things a little by explaining that, should one be able by any means to reach the roof of the building in which the parcel room was situated, and to let oneself down into the little garden and scale the railings unseen by the sentry, one would find oneself in the open street and free. It was intensely improbable that one could show oneself at all on the roof without being seen by at least one sentry; the chances of landing in, and crossing, that tiny brilliantly lit garden without being stopped or fired at were infinitesimal. The likelihood of a man being able to climb those railings and then jump into the street without being challenged either by another sentry or a passer-by was remote. Nevertheless this is what I decided to attempt, though the very thought of it made me shiver. The fact remains that I was at the end of my tether and I saw no other hope.

My first job was to find some way of getting into the quartermaster's stores, from whence I could, I believed, get out on to the roof. The sentry on the wire fence was authorized to allow prisoners through to visit the censor while he was at work, and this fact gave me access to the door of the QM's stores which, as I have said, was on the same landing as that of the censor's office. On the other hand, any efforts on my part to force this door would most certainly be heard by the censor and his staff. A lock can, however, be *picked* with scarcely any noise, and it therefore became apparent to me that I must depend on my skill in this direction to help me. There is nothing better for this purpose than the thin strong steel wire used for stiffening an ordinary officer's cap, and with this I made two implements and spent several days practising on any available locks within the camp. In this way I became very proficient and had perfect confidence in my ability to overcome this first difficulty.

I had decided that this time I would put my German to the test, and travel if possible by train. Indeed I had no other choice, for the weather was bitterly cold and I had before me a journey of three hundred miles. I had been warned that it would be fatal to travel openly within at least forty miles of the frontier, so I chose Bremen as my destination, it being a large town, and planned to go westwards on foot from there, and to try to cross into Holland through the marshes near the coast. As the day drew near I became very nervous. Only one friend, Captain Cutbill, of the Suffolk Regiment, knew what I was about, and I did not even tell Wasilief, for it was an impossible stunt for two, and I was afraid he would feel very much hurt at my trying without him. I used to lie awake at night thinking over the difficulties before me, and often I would picture myself cornered in the garden like an unfortunate rat, while a frightened and furious sentry blazed at me. It was a very dangerous undertaking (but probably not so dangerous as I imagined) and even should I succeed in breaking out of camp, my prospects of getting clear of Germany were hardly worth considering. Failing to reach Holland, I should be punished, inevitably be separated from my friends, and probably find myself later in a camp stronger, if possible, even than Halle. I was frankly terrified and would have given all I possessed to be able to renounce the whole affair with a clear conscience; but I could not, and for that I am very thankful.

The day arrived and I dressed myself in my room with the feelings of a condemned man. Over my civilian clothes I wore uniform, and carried with me some food, my compass and a small map of the country between Bremen and the Dutch frontier which I had been at some pains to obtain. It was about three o'clock in the afternoon and the sentry, on our producing a couple of letters ostensibly for the censor, allowed Cutbill and myself to pass through the wicket. We crept very, very quietly up the stairs, passed the censor's office on tiptoe and reached our door. I produced the two small wires and, inserting one in the lock, lifted the spring and showed my friend how to hold it braced. I knelt down and, pushing in the second wire, felt for the bolt. Twice my wire engaged and then, when I strained, slipped with a loud click. We both swore steadily under our breath, and I sweated, expecting every moment to hear the door behind us open, to look round and find some spotty little German clerk staring at us in astonishment. Once more I tried, and felt the wire now grip firmly into the slot. I pressed – pressed – and at last felt the bolt slide back and the door open under my hand. I got up and, slipping off my coat, handed it to my friend.

"Goodbye, old thing. Thanks frightfully."

"Goodbye; good luck! I wish to the Lord I was coming with you."

"I wish to Heaven you were!" I said, and moving into the room closed the door behind me and locked it again. I found the stores divided into two rooms, and had another locked door to tackle, but I made short work of this and began to take off the rest of my uniform in the little room in which I now found myself. So far everything had gone as well as I could possibly hope, and I now had to look about for some material to make a rope. There was nothing in this room which could possibly help me, although I had (most unwisely) depended on finding something there. If the worst came to the worst I should be obliged to tear my uniform into strips, but this did not seem at all a satisfactory solution, so I set to work on the lock of the second door again, and found in the other half of the stores a large bundle of leather straps, which would serve my purpose admirably. Having plaited several of these together to form a rope, I sat down to wait for darkness. Extraordinary though it may seem when one remembers the exceedingly unpleasant task which lay before me, I managed to have a sleep, and on waking amused myself by reading some very ancient German newspapers. Suddenly, about five o'clock, I heard a key in the lock of the outer door. Oh, Lord! they knew then? The sentry must have reported to his relief that I was with the censor and, on my not returning, inquiries must have been made, in which case they would know that I was hiding somewhere in the building. In horrible anxiety I knelt and peeped through the keyhole, and there to my immense relief saw a German N.C.O. in charge of a party of orderlies, who were engaged in carrying bedsteads out of the room. There was a small window in my compartment which looked out on the courtyard of the camp, and from here I could see my friend gazing at the building with a comical, troubled look on his face, evidently thinking that I had been caught.

The fatigue party did not remain there to worry me for long, for I heard them depart, locking the door behind them. I noticed that it was raining, though not heavily, and this distressed me, for I had not been able to obtain a greatcoat, try as I would. About half-past six it was getting dusk and the lights were turned on, for the Germans here, as I have said, were remarkably careful and gave away no chances. By seven o'clock it would have been dark but for the arc-lamps, and I judged that the moment had come. I am afraid my hands were not very steady as I pulled a couple of large boxes into the middle of the room and putting one on top of the other reached the skylight. I pushed it open and then, giving a vigorous kick, did a sort of "both hands leading" and scrambled out on to the roof. In a moment I was back again and had closed the skylight behind me. It was *impossible*. I had never realized before how impossible it was. The fact that prisoners were not able to approach near to the sentries' beat had prevented my appreciating the fact that at least three of them had a direct view of my roof. There was an arc-lamp on the roof; it was as bright as day up there, and probably I had already been seen. I stood there dumbfounded and feeling absolutely desperate. I had burned my boats behind me with a vengeance, for no one was allowed in the parcel room or censor's office after 4 p.m., and I should be arrested and everything would be discovered if I tried to get back. What on earth should I do? The others would think I had funked it, and I *did* funk it, for it looked like suicide. In my despair I prayed for help, though God knows what help I expected. Outside it was raining – by Jove, it was raining – such a sudden downpour as I have seldom seen. I had no coat, I thought; if I were out in it I should be drenched. Everybody would be drenched. The sentries would – O-o-oh! the sentries would be in their boxes! Slowly it dawned upon me that the answer to my prayer had come, and then I jumped for it. In a moment my hands were gripping the edge of the skylight – set teeth and a heave, and I was on the roof. Not a soul was to be seen in the courtyard of the camp; every sentry was in his box. I stood up on the roof in the deluge, fixed my rope, pulled once heavily upon it, and then, throwing myself clear of the gutter, slid down. I landed with a bump not more than four yards from the sentry, who stood in his box, and ran down to the railings. Every moment I expected to hear a shout behind me, but my man had bowed his head to the beating rain and had seen nothing. The railings were easy – much easier than I had anticipated; just one short scramble and I was in the street. There was no one about; I had not been seen, and, turning to the left I ran off with my head in a whirl. I had gone perhaps a hundred yards when I stopped for an instant and looked back. I could scarcely believe what I had done. Those blazing lights – those masses of barbed wire – those dogs and sentries – they had all been of no avail to hold me. I was soaked to the skin and very cold, I had no friend and nowhere to lay my head, but I had done it! I was in a state of indescribable elation. And so I looked on Halle camp for the last, last time, and sped on.

Chapter Six

I had hoped most earnestly to be able to break out without giving myself away, and had intended to tie a stone to the end of the rope, and throw it back on to the roof, where it would not be noticed till daylight. I had, however, landed very much nearer the sentry than I had expected, and could not possibly take the risk of delaying, though I now realized that the moment the man left his shelter he would see the rope and give the alarm. The rain had ceased, and I must therefore take it for granted that he had already done so, and that the fact of my escape was known. There were several people about in the streets again, and I dared not run, though I realized that my whole object must be to get away quickly from Halle, no matter in which direction. I felt myself a very suspicious figure, dripping wet as I was and, for one moment, hesitated at the entrance to the station; but it was the only way, so nerving myself up, I hurried to the booking office, and asked for a fourth class ticket to Berlin. The clerk came forward to his little window and looked me up and down. He drummed his fingers on the ledge, paused, and then asked me:

"What are you going to Berlin for?"

For a moment I thought of saying I was going there to work, but I saw the trap in time, for, had this been the case, I should have been provided with a paper entitling me to a rebate of fare.

"My father has died," I answered, "and I have only just time to get to his funeral."

He stamped out my ticket at once, and I went up on to the platform. I have hitherto omitted to say that, during my journey from Augustabad and on all subsequent stunts, I invariably assumed a terrific limp and had acquired the art of half-closing one eye while I opened the other in a glassy stare. This gave me a truly awful aspect, and was doubly enough to account for my freedom from military service, though I need not say that this grimace, among my friends, was considered to be a great improvement on my normal appearance.

I had not long to wait before a train came in, and I had no difficulty in finding an empty fourth class compartment, into which I jumped. I was feeling wonderfully happy as the train slid out of the station, although I had no idea in which direction it was taking me. All I knew was that I must get away from Halle before the camp authorities telephoned my description to the station police, and this I was doing. For an hour and a half I travelled alone with my thoughts, and then, at a place called Cuten, the train stopped, and an inspector got in and examined my ticket. He made a great fuss when he found I was in the wrong train, yelling at me and calling me a young imbecile, and told me that I should have to buy another ticket back to Halle, that being my only way to Berlin. The idea immediately crossed my mind that he knew who I was, that this was merely a ruse to get me back to my starting point, and that I should find an escort waiting for me there. I did not, however, dare to refuse for fear of still more rousing his suspicions, so obtained another ticket, and allowed myself to be pushed into a carriage full of soldiers. I had not, of course, the slightest intention of showing myself again in Halle, so sat well back in my seat while we stopped there, and then let the train take me on to Leipzig, further than which it did not go. And here a new difficulty arose, for it was clear to me that any attempt to pass the barrier with my wrong tickets would give rise to a lengthy discussion, in which I would not, probably, be able to disguise my nationality. One ticket was from Halle to Berlin, the other was from Cuten to Halle, and here was I at midnight in Leipzig!

There were not many people left in the station with the exception of officials, so that I began to feel myself somewhat conspicuous. I had some cigarettes which I had bought on the platform, but no matches, and feeling that I simply *must* have a smoke I got down on to the line, and was trying to light my cigarette off the tail-lamp of a train, when an angry shout stopped me. A porter started to abuse me for touching the lamp, and a policeman, strolling past, stopped to listen and then suddenly asked me for my papers. I at once produced my tickets, and the confusion which arose over them drove the matter of the papers out of his mind. A little crowd started to form, and several theories were put forward as to what I was, the general opinion being that I was halfwitted. This, of course, suited me down to the ground, but I judged it as well to harrow their feelings with the story of my recent bereavement. This I did with great success, and when I reached the part where, with only a few marks in my pocket and not even a greatcoat to my back, I leave my work and set out in the pouring rain, in order to be in time for one last look at "the father", I carried my audience with me. Yes, they were Germans, and to the best of their knowledge I was one of them. Had they known what I really was, I do not doubt that the scene would have been a very different one, but the fact remains that they gave me their sympathy, and I give them in return a little credit.

They led me off to the barrier, and there the whole story was recited to the ticket inspector, who accepted my tickets, as they more than covered the journey I had made and told me that I should be able to get a train to Bremen at 5 a.m. I went off highly satisfied, and sat down in a large general waiting-room, where I found it slightly warmer than on the platform. There were only ten or twelve people in the place, including a young man whom I should imagine to have been a tout of some description. This fellow, evidently thinking I was a simple country youngster, tried to borrow ten marks from me, but he was interrupted by the arrival of a policeman, who demanded to see everybody's passports.

This was awful! My only hope was to refer him to the inspector, and this I intended to do, though with small hopes of its satisfying him, when suddenly a diversion occurred. The policeman had almost reached me, when he noticed that one of the company, a labouring man, was drunk. Having examined his papers, he told him roughly to leave the station and to come back when he was sober. Objections were raised, and a truly German shouting match commenced, in the course of which some remark, which I was unable to catch, so stung to fury the strong arm of the law that it reached out and seized my saviour by the scruff of the neck. A short struggle ensued, and then, almost lifting him by the collar, the policeman started to run him across the hall. Twice, using his legs as props to stay his progress, the prisoner flung them forward, but each time was carried over them. In a last glimpse I saw him, with legs spread out and braced against each side of the door, while the policeman strove mightily ... It was enough for me, and I limped to the other end of the station, determined to avoid that constable at all costs!

At five o'clock the following morning I found myself in the train bound for Bremen. I had my ticket all correct, and was told to my relief that I would not have to change, so that bar accidents or another demand for papers I was all right. There were about fifteen other people in the carriage, mostly women, and there was one whole family complete even to the mother in law, who nagged the unfortunate father unceasingly. The talk ran practically entirely on food and food prices, but there was astonishingly little grumbling – just an air of resignation. They spoke of Verdun with long faces. One had a brother there and another a son, and it was all very terrible, but would soon be over of course. Verdun would fall and then Paris, but whether it would be necessary to invade England they did not know. Anyway, it would all come right in the end – Hindenburg had said so, and when our Hindenburg said anything – na – der schafft es!

We pulled up in a large station and I leant my head out of the window, only to pull it in again with such haste as might almost have drawn suspicion on me. Halle again! Was I never to be free of the place? I began to fear that the train might be searched, but the thought of my roundabout journey came to reassure me. Two men got into the carriage and started a lengthy discussion as to how they could best swindle their employer out of three marks, which had been left over after some deal with which they had been entrusted. This was settled to our great edification, and I fell asleep for a short time. It was an uneventful journey on the whole, and my chief recollection of it is that I was very cold, for I was still wet and my dungarees were miserably thin. Every mile brought me nearer the frontier, and one would think that the knowledge of this would have sufficed to make me indifferent to physical discomfort; but every mile brought me nearer the decision and I dreaded it.

Thinking the matter over, I have come to the conclusion that this was the most difficult stunt I have ever tried. I was very poorly equipped both in map and compass and in clothing, I had no knowledge of the ground over which I had to cross, and no information whatever as regards the frontier. I am still convinced that it would have been impossible for two to have broken out together as I had done, but it has been generally agreed among prisoners of experience that it is almost always hopeless to try alone. A man needs some sort of company under such difficult circumstances.

It was six o'clock in the evening before we ran into Bremen, and my thirteen hours travelling had left me stiff and tired. No papers were demanded at the barrier and I passed out with the crowd into the street, and then hesitated, for I had no idea which direction to take. Imagine yourself dumped down in the middle of Liverpool and told to walk out of the town without asking the way of anybody, and you will then have a conception of the position in which I found myself, for although my German was fluent, I could not sustain a long conversation and must do all in my power to prevent being spoken to. I went into a shop and bought some apples, for I was hungry and had not been able to bring much food with me. Biscuits would have suited me far better, but I was none too sure of the German word; also I did not know whether they could be bought without coupons, and it was essential not to display ignorance in these matters. So I ate my apples and precious little good did they do me.

I then started off to tramp the streets, trying as much as I could to keep in one direction, but dared not keep looking at my compass and found myself walking in circles. Sometimes I would walk about a mile, only to finish up on some wharf and have to retrace my steps again. There was an east wind blowing and a few flakes of snow fell and lay unmelted on the ground. I began to feel very done and horribly cold, also I was completely lost, and the feeling was slowly being borne in on me that I had shot my bolt and could never succeed now. It was that first part – it had been too hard – had taken too much out of me ... I bit a piece of chocolate and smashed a tooth, and then, biting on the piece of tooth, set all the rest on edge. God hated me!

By nine that night I was no nearer getting away than when I had started. Had I been able to go to some very cheap lodging-house and spend the night in bed, I should perhaps have been capable of tackling the job the following morning, but to do this one needed papers, so it was out of the question. Seeing a tram marked "Bahnhof", I got in and returned to the station, for, risky though it might be, I had decided to travel by train still further westwards to a town called Delmenhorst, which was marked on my map. I should be able to rest a little in the train, and hoped to find at Delmenhorst some place where I could spend the night, so got my ticket, and, having a wait of half an hour before me, made my way to a waiting-room, and tried to warm myself against a radiator. I was very sorry when the time came to quit this – the only warm spot I had found since leaving my room in the camp – but I could not afford to miss the train. There were a crowd of young munition workers and one or two surprisingly pretty girls in the compartment into which I got, but I was in no mood to appreciate feminine beauty and, on one of them starting to chaff me, I told my story, which I knew now almost by heart. Everybody respected my filial grief, and I had no further trouble.

It was midnight before we reached Delmenhorst and I passed safely out of the station and started off down the road. A girl was walking in front of me, but as I caught up on her she gave a little subdued scream and broke into a run. It almost amused me that any-one should be frightened of *me* at that time. It was pitch dark, and, my compass not being luminous, I was obliged to strike matches (of which I had bought a box in Bremen) in order to set my map. But the wind had considerably increased, and I found it most difficult to keep the flame going long enough for more than a glance at the instrument. After having covered about four miles in, roughly, a westerly direction without finding any place where I could sleep, I at last passed a small cottage, behind which stood some sheds. I left the road, and was trying with numb fingers to open one of the shed doors, when I heard a dog bark in the house, and then the sound of a man's voice. Running round to get clear of the house, I saw, standing in the doorway, a man; he held a lighted lamp in one hand, while with the other he restrained a large dog, and I turned and bolted stumbling down the road.

My only hope now appeared to be to return to the town. On my way there I left the road to explore everything that looked like a barn, but – and the cold and exhausted know these illusions well – in every case my eyes had played me false, and what had promised to be my night's lodging was no more than a distant copse. Then I would tramp back over the frozen ploughland until I struck the road again. By now I was dropping with sleep, yet dare not lie down exposed on such a night. I reached Delmenhorst again and got into the churchyard, but the church was closed, and I could find no proper shelter of any sort. Thence back to the station, only to find it shut, and to discover that it would not be open again until 9 a.m. From there I set off again with scarcely any idea but to keep myself warm, although it must have been clear to me that I was much too exhausted to continue on the move for another seven hours. After a certain amount of blind wandering in the dark, I found myself on the railway line. Following it up I reached the station, and then climbed up on to the platform and looked to see if there were any fires in the waiting-rooms. There were none. The only sign of warmth I saw was a stove burning brightly in the telegraph office, the door of which stood open, and here I hesitated, looking longingly at the blaze. The room was empty, and, persuading myself that I would only stop there long enough to warm my hands, I went in.

Remember, I make no excuses, nor do I wish to hide the fact that I knew this to be so dangerous as to be almost equivalent to surrender. It maddens me, even as I write, to think of the amount of energy I had expended to get so far – of the colossal luck which had been mine – and then to remember how I threw all my chances to the winds for lack of a little courage against the cold. Perhaps had I turned then and pushed on ... But I didn't, and I paid for it.

I do not think I had been there for more than a few seconds when a railway official, coming into the room, stopped with a jerk at the door, and looked me up and down in astonishment. "Um Gottes Willen, woher dann?" said he.

I stood there like a fool, my hands stretched out to the blaze, straining to keep my eyes open, for the heat had made me even more sleepy than before, and I made no answer. As a matter of fact I was racking my brain to remember whether "woher" meant "where to" or "where from," but, totally unable to collect my thoughts, I had to give it up, and said slowly:

"If you'll give me a minute to get warm, I'll tell you all about it."

I recollect that I made, in this simple sentence, at least two mistakes, and was not at all surprised when he moved towards the door, saying:

"All right, you can sleep here for a bit."

I looked round and saw a closed window behind me. This offered me still a means of escape, but I had absolutely no energy left in me, and I felt that I did not care a straw what happened now. I watched the key turning over slowly in the lock, for he thought he was being very clever – this amateur Sherlock Holmes.

"I suppose you are going to ring up the police now?" I called out.

"Yes, you're an escaped Russian prisoner," came the answer. "Remember, I am armed!"

"No," I said, "I'm a British officer," and then I just threw myself down on the floor before the stove and fell asleep.

I suppose I had slept for about ten minutes when I was rudely awakened by finding myself suddenly hauled up on to my feet. Two policemen had come to fetch me, and they started searching me at once, being so unnecessarily rough about it that the official, who stood looking on, remarked:

"Steady, steady, he says he's an officer, you know."

By now they had opened my shirt, and having examined my identity disc their treatment of me improved considerably. I was still half asleep as they led me off to the local police prison – too sleepy to realize properly what a hopeless failure I had made of my chances. I was taken into a cell and made to undress there. A British officer was, I suppose, rather a curiosity in those days, and much to my disgust several people stood watching me at the door, including two wardresses. I was only too glad to lie down on the straw mattress in my cell, and though very cold, for they had deprived me of all but my shirt, I made what shift I could, wrapping the single blanket round me, and was soon asleep again.

I woke up the following morning very hungry and badly in need of a cigarette. For breakfast I got some acorn coffee with neither milk nor sugar, and nothing whatever to eat. I asked the gaoler if he would give me one of the cigarettes which had been taken from me, but found him obdurate and very uncivil, so I would not humiliate myself by pressing the point. My lunch consisted of a bowl of cabbage soup and a slice of bread, of which I left not a crumb, and I spent the afternoon walking up and down my cell, thinking over every detail of the whole affair. I was completely at a loss to understand my behaviour of the night before, and indeed I have never understood it to this day. It would be impossible to exaggerate the disgust I felt in myself, or the intensity of my regret, and the only explanation which I could offer myself was that the average man is capable of sustaining just a certain amount of physical and mental strain, and that beyond this point he cannot carry on. It was none the less terrible to me to think that I was returning the following day to the town I had left so triumphantly only a short while before, and returning with my tail between my legs. I saw little prospect for the future, for I was a marked man now, and my chances, if they ever came again, would be very few and very far between. Of two things I was determined – I would not lie about the circumstances of my recapture and, secondly, I swore to myself that never, never again, whilst there was one single chance left to me, would I give up hope.

I slept little that night, and was glad when my cell door was opened early the following morning and I was told that the escort had arrived to take me back to Halle. The under-officer having satisfied himself that I had nothing about me which could possibly be of assistance to me in escaping, delivered himself of the usual warning and we set off for the station. It was plain to me that these men had received very careful instructions as to their method of guarding me, for they kept always to the same formation – one in front of me and the other behind, and they did not sling their rifles as is generally done, but carried them ready for any emergency. Our journey in the train was uneventful, though one small incident occurred to relieve the monotony. A Feldwebel, on leave from the Verdun fighting, got into the carriage, and thinking I was just an ordinary civilian embarked on a most graphic description of his experiences there. His company had, it appeared, suffered the most severe losses – half the men shell shocked – and the long and short of it was that flesh and blood simply could not—! He was interrupted by one of my guard, who had been signalling to him unobserved for some time.

"Steady on, steady on," he said, "this is an Englishman."

I have seldom seen a man more astonished or annoyed, and from then on, to relieve his feelings, I suppose, he continued to heap abuse on England and the English. Any remarks of mine merely served to make him more insulting, and I relapsed into silence. Conceive me sitting there, red-faced with fury and humiliation, yet completely impotent – I, who had thought to have the laugh of these beasts before the week was out!

On our arrival at Halle station, an N.C.O. from the camp met us with the order that we were to proceed straight to the military prison. On our way there we met the Adjutant of the camp, who pretended to be intensely amused at the sight of me. I was very dirty and had several days' growth on my chin, but I cannot think that I was a fit subject for such roars of laugher as he indulged in, there in the street.

"Ach, *so*, Herr Leutnant," he said, "your journey has not lasted quite so long as you expected," and then in the true German manner – for one often wonders if their laughter is *ever* genuine – he grew suddenly biting and cried, "Why for have you done it?

I tell you that it is in order that you may say you have escaped from Halle. Es ist ganz zwecklos gewesen. No prisoner can escape from us!"

"March!" said he, and clicked his heels as I saluted.

We arrived at the prison and I was taken over by the Feldwebel in charge and locked up in a cell between a German officer, who had been sentenced to three months for sending false dispatches with the object of gaining a decoration, and a Russian lieutenant, who had forged the name of a friend on a canteen chit. Of the German officer one did not of course see much but, as the Feldwebel allowed us a lot of freedom in the prison courtyard, the Russian was my constant companion during a month, and a description of him may not, therefore, be amiss.

He was short and fair, with the true Russian eyes – not pouchy like those of a Chinaman, but set at a peculiar slant in his face. He had a great mass of curly fair hair, and a little beard, parted in the middle, and I should judge him to have been about twenty four, though he always maintained that he was nineteen. He was, in all things, a consistent and incurable liar. He made no secret of the charge on which he was awaiting trial, and after the first two days of our acquaintance, did not even bother to deny it, but told me the full details of the affair. I must frankly admit that it did not trouble me in the least, and we agreed that we would not discuss it again while we were together.

What property I had left behind me was sent from the camp, and my civilian clothes were of course confiscated. I had a certain amount of money in my account with the camp paymaster, and this was handed over to the Feldwebel. In this way I was able to repay him for any risk he might run in allowing us more time for exercise than we were strictly entitled to.

Outside the prison yard, which was surrounded by a twelve-foot brick wall, were some allotments, and very often an old man who worked here would mount a ladder and watch us from over the top of the wall. He had, I remember, lost three fingers during the war of 1870, and he had also been wounded in 1866. This old fellow had a goat of which he was inordinately proud, and the goat appeared to be just about all he had in the world. One morning we saw him crying, and he told us with a trembling lip that his goat had died in the night while kidding, at which we were immensely distressed, and went in to find the Feldwebel. We persuaded him to give us thirty marks each out of our accounts, and this we presented to the old man, handing the notes up to him tied on to a broom, amidst the plaudits of Madame Feldwebel. The suggestion had come from the Russian, and it made me realize how very careful one must be before one sits in judgment, for he had very little money at that time and could ill afford to do what he had done. One would like to think that the Recording Angel was moved to blot out the mark against his name.

I was a month in prison at Halle and things were made very much easier for me by the English in the camp, who had sent me down a box full of tinned food and some books, which the Germans allowed me to have. Apropos of this, it is perhaps a fact worth recording that the more trouble I gave, the more respect was shown me by my captors, and though their treatment of me became in time very stringent, it was not often, after my first year of captivity, that I was exposed to insult. All this was, I suppose, in accordance with the nature of the German.

Two charges, in addition to that of having broken out, were preferred against me. First, of having made use of skeleton keys, and, secondly, of having stolen the straps with which I made my rope. Neither of these charges was pressed for lack of evidence, and I was informed that I should therefore be transferred to Magdeburg Camp. I had heard little good of this place, but it offered at least a better chance than the prison, and it was with a new feeling of hope and excitement that I fell in with the escort for our march to the station.

Chapter Seven

"Halt! Herr Unteroffizier, Ich möchte ihre Papiere nachsehen!" We had marched about half a mile from Magdeburg Station, and had been halted by a sentry on a bridge over the railway. The N.C.O. in charge of the escort produced his papers, and we crossed the bridge and followed the road down into the camp. This road was apparently the only legitimate means of entrance and exit. It was fenced on both sides with high barbed wire entanglements and we were halted three times before we reached the gates of the camp. Two German soldiers passed us, leading five or six large police dogs, and I began to realize that this was a place where the Germans knew their business, and did it!

An old fort named after a Prussian general of long ago – a new mobilization store called the Wagenhaus; the two included in one great circle of barbed wire fences and high wooden wire-topped palings; here a dry moat; there two high mounds from which a Landsturm man with slung rifle looked down upon the camp; sentries, sentries everywhere, and down in the middle of it all many prisoners of many nationalities walked idly to and fro; Magdeburg as I saw it at a first glance.

I was handed over to the corporal of the guard, who in turn took me straight to the orderly room. Here my particulars were taken, and a description of myself was made out and filed, much to my chagrin. I was shown the room in which I was to sleep, and given a few minutes to make myself known to the other prisoners there. The room held about thirty officers, ten of whom were English. Here they slept and here they had their meals. Several were Frenchmen whom I had previously known at Halle, and they in their usual way gave me a great welcome, and showed genuine delight on hearing that I had at last succeeded in breaking out. It had always been greatly resented by the prisoners that Halle should be a virgin camp, as we called it, and of this it could no longer boast. While I was talking a Belgian of the name of Baschwitz whom I had also known slightly at Halle came into the room and joined the group. A man in a thousand this – short and slim and muscular, about thirty, with blue eyes, a turned-up moustache, a fine chin, and possessed of a most acute sense of humour. He had spent most of his life in Africa and South America, and spoke fluent English and perfect German, for he had been six years at school in Berlin. He had as I knew made various attempts to get out of Halle, but each time had met with failure. He was the real soul of adventure, this man; nothing in life could satisfy his craving for excitement and danger, and I knew that he felt his captivity indescribably. I found that I was addressing my whole story to him and, though perhaps one did not know it at the time, a real understanding sprang up between us in those few short minutes which was destined to be a lasting one.

I was interrupted by the arrival of a clerk from the orderly room, who said that the Commandant wished to see me there at once. I found him seated at his desk – a typical Prussian colonel in his old style red and blue uniform. He was short and thick with a huge neck, quite bald, with a heavy moustache and a loose jowl, and he glared at me through strong glasses. "Ach, you are the Leutenant Hardy, yes? You are from Halle, yes? from where you have escaped, yes, no? I say to you, from here *can* you not escape! If you even make the try you will be shot against the wall. Verstechen Sie? Jetzt konnen Sie gehen."

I was furious at being threatened in this manner in the presence of the whole orderly room personnel, but I had no choice but to remain silent, for I could not run the risk of bringing fresh punishment on myself at this time. This indeed was a point which I had always to consider. Many prisoners seemed to derive a certain amount of satisfaction out of constantly irritating the Germans and breaking small regulations. We, who had scarcely any thought beyond escape, were obliged most carefully to avoid these minor offences, for they invariably resulted in constant interruptions in our efforts.

Having been dismissed by the Colonel, I went down into the courtyard and strolled round that part of the camp to which the prisoners had access. It was not long before I had satisfied myself that this was going to be a very difficult proposition. The side of the camp upon which the fort lay did not appear to offer any possibilities at all. I had myself seen the care which was exercised to identify persons entering or leaving the camp, and I was convinced that no disguise could be perfect enough to succeed without the necessary papers. I must therefore turn my attention to the Wagenhaus end of the camp, and I was walking across when I was joined by Baschwitz. Well, what did I think of it? Oh, I thought it was infernally hard, but I wasn't going to give up hope for a long time yet. After all, I had thought Halle impossible, but I had managed it somehow or other, and that had given me a deuce of a lot of confidence. Yes, well, he'd had great hopes at Magdeburg, but every time he had got started on anything the Germans had seemed to get started on it too and barred the way. Gradually the camp had become so hard that he had begun to lose hope. But two heads were better than one, and perhaps between us—? You bet! So we agreed to spend the next twenty four hours investigating everything that looked like offering us a chance, and then to meet again and compare ideas. In accordance with this resolution I spent a long time at various points of vantage about the camp, and went to bed with three separate schemes slowly maturing in my mind.

Evening roll call took place about nine o'clock, and the prisoners were obliged to be in bed for this most solemn ceremony. I was anxious to see what precautions were taken by the Germans, for I knew that should I ever succeed in breaking out of Magdeburg, they, knowing my previous history, would immediately communicate with the railway authorities. Should they do this my chance of success would be small indeed unless I had a start of several hours, and this could only be obtained by "faking" the roll call. I therefore covered my head with the blanket on this first night, and lying perfectly still pretended to be asleep. The officer paused at my bed and told the sentry to make sure that I was not a dummy. This was said laughingly, for the Germans in their hearts were convinced that escape from Magdeburg was impossible, but it left a nasty taste in my mouth! These people were going to be very difficult to deal with, I thought, but nevertheless one was becoming more cunning daily and one would have a splendid man to work with – desperately keen, obviously courageous – and with these thoughts I fell asleep.

We had to be out at eight o'clock each morning for roll call, which took place in the courtyard. The officers of each room fell in in a separate group, and were supposed to be in fours. Various sentries were posted in order to prevent their moving from one group to the other. As soon as we had been dismissed we went upstairs and cooked our breakfast, and after this meal I went off to find Baschwitz, who lived in a room on the other side of the passage. I found him shaving, and as soon as he had finished we went down and sat on a bench in the sun, lit our cigarettes, and I then laid my three plans before him. Two of them, with his superior knowledge of the camp, he was able to veto at the outset, but the third had already occurred to him as a possibility, though he had small hopes of its ever succeeding. However, we were absolutely determined to make an attempt, and the place which I am about to describe appeared to be the one and only weak spot in the whole defences of the camp.

Behind the Wagenhaus was a very small triangular courtyard in which a sentry was stationed night and day, and into which no officer was ever allowed to go. One side of the triangle was formed by the usual double barbed wire fence, the second side was formed by the end of the building, and the third consisted of a ten foot wooden paling, along the top of which had been fixed curved iron stanchions carrying barbed wire. Access to the yard was gained by a door in the building, and against the wooden fence had been built a small latrine for the use of the orderlies and the German soldiers. No officer, as I have said, was allowed here.

It was useless to consider trying to scale the entanglement, for it was very high, and not a mouse could have moved in the courtyard without being seen by the sentry. On the other hand, if once in the latrine and able to work there uninterrupted, it would be possible to cut a hole in the paling sufficiently large to crawl through. Parallel to, and outside the paling, ran a low railway embankment along which sentries were posted. One of the latter was unfortunately placed precisely opposite the point where one would emerge. It was difficult at first to see any imaginable combination of circumstances which could make this enterprise feasible. In the first place we must be sufficiently well disguised to deceive the sentry into the belief that we were orderlies; this did not appear so difficult; but in the second place we must be absolutely safe from disturbance while cutting through the paling, and to make sure of this we must do it at night, when the yard was closed and no one allowed to use the latrine. Yes, but how were we to get there? Oh, Lord! I'd forgotten that – what a fool I was! We sat there in the deepest thought. For the moment I saw no way out of the difficulty, and was just going to suggest that we should go and make another examination of the courtyard from a window in the Wagenhaus, when suddenly Baschwitz caught me by the arm.

"I know how we do it! "he cried. "We hide in the latrine in the day and wait till it is dark, and as for the evening roll call we must – how you say?"

"Fake it, by Jove!" I shouted, and then looked round uneasily to see if anyone had heard me.

And now for the sentry on the embankment – how on earth to avoid him? He could not possibly fail to see us unless he had walked right off his beat, and this he never did. When he was in the box— By the Lord! his box faced sideways to the paling, and when he was in it there was a good chance he would not see us. If it were raining heavily he would certainly take shelter, and *there* was the key to the whole affair. We must hide there during the day; we must break out at night when it was raining. We got up flushed and excited at having solved our problem so far satisfactorily. We were in the highest imaginable spirits. Much work was still to be done, but we felt we were undoubtedly on the right path.

Baschwitz had been nearly eight months at Magdeburg and consequently had many friends there. The task, therefore, of getting together the necessary clothes, etc. (for we had nothing) fell practically entirely on his shoulders, and indeed he was very much better qualified to deal with it than I was, for he had a most persuasive way about him. Many of the prisoners wore dungaree trousers, and one Belgian officer wore a pair of civilian ones with a red stripe sewn down the leg, and these we coveted beyond all others. On the other hand, one was unwilling to suggest an exchange with these people until one was just about to make the attempt, for it was impossible that they should not suspect our intentions; and nothing could be more fatal than that our plans should be discussed by other prisoners. This meant leaving much to be done at the last moment and added a lot to our anxiety.

I left Baschwitz to start making inquiries about our outfits and made my way to a Russian room, where I had heard gambling was constantly in progress. There was a large crowd round the table, but I managed to squeeze myself in and take a hand. I had very little money and was anxious to get some quickly, for an Englishman had offered me a twenty mark note if I should need it, and I wished to be able to pay him at once. I have often noticed that when one desires to win money for some particular object one rarely succeeds, and I remember that on this occasion I lost every cent I had. However, I managed to get some money from a friend and gave him a cheque for the amount. I then went off and bought the note, though the Englishman was unwilling to take payment for it. In many camps the *moral* was very high, and the comradeship and generosity among prisoners, especially in the matter of helping one another in escape stunts, really made one feel sometimes that captivity was almost worth while. The Englishman of whom I have spoken was out of place in Magdeburg, for it was not such a camp. Many of the prisoners there had doubtless had a hard time, though treatment had improved before I arrived. Their discomforts may have served to make them somewhat sour, but it is a fact that one was made to feel oneself not quite a gentleman! It simply was not *done* to be breaking out of camps and travelling about Germany dressed like a tramp; and all this conspiring with a foreigner was a great mistake.

Oh, you Magdeburgers! Forgive me if I am spiteful – but I deal this little smack not only in my own name but in the name of two others who, like me, suffered a little under your witticisms, but who had the laugh of you in the end.

Chapter Eight

On the stairs leading up to my room there was a landing with a window, and from here one could watch any movements in the courtyard which had so aroused our interest. We could have stood here looking out the whole day, and indeed would have done so in the hope of gleaning some new piece of information, but that we feared to draw attention on ourselves. The tendency constantly to watch that part of a camp which one has chosen as the scene of one's attempt is very strong, and has necessarily to be combated. In one fort in which I spent a large part of my captivity, the sentries had instructions to make a note of the name of any officer who was seen paying special attention to any particular part of the place, and in this way the Germans were kept aware of practically every scheme on foot and many plans were thus frustrated at the outset.

Baschwitz and I scarcely allowed ourselves more than a glance in passing, though this we managed to do very often, and before long had, I think, grasped every detail which could be of interest to us. We were, however, very anxious to know exactly what went on there at nights, and this was more difficult to ascertain, for such were the precautions taken by the Germans that a sentry was stationed on the landing between evening and morning roll calls. In what capacity he functioned I have never been able to imagine, nor what he was supposed to prevent, for a jump into the yard would merely have landed one into the arms of the sentry below, and even then one's difficulties would only have begun. However, there he stood, and an infernal nuisance he was. One night I came out of my room and, after having walked up and down the corridor for some time, went down on to the landing and engaged him in conversation. I offered him some tobacco, and while he was transferring it to his pouch managed to get a view of the yard for a few seconds. Then I bade him good night and going back to my room sat there on the bed in the dark, and thought miserably over what I had seen. I did not know what poor Baschwitz would say when I told him, indeed I almost feared to break the news to him – for all our surmises were incorrect and we were verily undone! In this camp, unlike most others, rounds were done every hour by an officer accompanied by a N.C.O. and a couple of sentries with police dogs. Every post was visited and we had not thought it probable that even the sentry in our little yard would be excepted. But that they would go the length of entering the latrine and making sure that no prisoner had hidden himself there had never occurred to us. Yet this was what I had seen them doing, and it was obvious to me that the Germans were on their guard against just such a scheme as we had evolved.

In the morning I told Baschwitz, and for hours we walked gloomily round the camp, discussing the affair over and over again, but we saw no way out of the difficulty, for the thing could not possibly be done by day owing to the constant flow of Germans and orderlies to the latrine. Those were very bad days indeed, for we were practically at a standstill. Baschwitz pushed on halfheartedly with his arrangements for obtaining civilian clothes, should we need them, and also constantly studied an old timetable which he had stolen on some visit to the orderly room. I tried steadily to develop various other schemes, but absolutely without success. I was not without ideas, but every single scheme turned out to have some grave flaw in it as soon as one made investigation. It was maddening, for we were both prepared to take a big risk, but the very defences of the camp seemed strong enough, without considering the rifles of the sentries. There was a very old Belgian officer in the camp who used to amuse himself by carpentering. He had certain simple tools, and we had previously persuaded him to ask the Germans if they would let him buy a small keyhole saw for cabinet-making. Nobody could have suspected this very aged and respectable gentleman of any ulterior motive, and they had consented. At last the saw had arrived and had been handed over to us, but it did not appear now that we should ever be able to put it to the use for which it had been intended. Another friend of Baschwitz's had a small amount of plaster of paris, for he was a sculptor by trade, and the Germans had allowed him to order this from the town. Baschwitz had got hold of a little of this, and had started to make a dummy face. Roll call in his room was not done nearly so thoroughly as in mine, and he was of the opinion that should we ever get clear of the camp he would be able to deceive the Germans at least till the following morning – that is of course if the dummy in his bed were sufficiently realistic. I, for my part, had obtained sixty marks in English money and had arranged with a Russian officer to exchange his jacket for my overcoat, should the necessity arise. This jacket was of the type issued about that time to Russian troops, and a few alterations would make it look quite civilian. All this was done, however, in a half-hearted spirit, and only that we might not be unprepared should any chance offer itself. But the days dragged on and nothing came.

Jutland! and then K.'s death at sea ... [May and June 1916] One walked round the camp with a long face in those days. They'd killed our best man, and faced our Navy, and – they hadn't been destroyed. Some people would not take it seriously – just laughed and said it was all lies. I don't think they did much good, for it is possible to be so very optimistic, dreadfully cheery, that you merely drive your companions to the other extreme. No, things were going just as badly as they possibly could, and we were doing nothing – *nothing* to help! I used to visit Baschwitz in his room and sit gloomily on his bed while he worked away at his dummy. It had certainly grown to be a wonderful bit of work, with a pink complexion, an aquiline nose and a fine head of hair, made of clippings from the barber's shop. It was a horrible looking object with its closed eyes and turned-up moustache, but was very much more gentlemanly in appearance than many of the prisoners – also, it did not spit!

About a week after we had received the news of Jutland I was informed one day that some Russians were about to make an attempt to escape. Russians were always just about to do this, but it was not often that they got beyond a public declaration to this effect. There was, however, the possibility that this might be no false alarm, and as an escape invariably leads to a general search, we had to look round for some hiding place for the dummy and such other *verbotene* articles as we possessed. We spent an hour searching the place for a likely spot, but, finding nothing, we were driven to the expedient of cutting through and raising one of the floor-boards in Baschwitz's room. There is always a certain amount of space between a floor and the ceiling of the room below, and this would suit us admirably. We had been engaged on this work for about half an hour and had unavoidably made a certain amount of noise, when a German under-officer entered the room. It was useless to cease work, for it was obvious what we had been doing, so we continued; or rather I should say Baschwitz continued, for it was he who was working at the moment. The under-officer watched us for some time and then left the room, returning in a few moments with the officer in charge of the block, and he, ordering the N.C.O. to see that we did not quit the building, went off to fetch the Commandant. The latter was exceedingly angry when he arrived, though he was at a loss to discover with what object the work had been done. Baschwitz explained that he was merely trying to cut a groove in which to fit the edge of the iron plate on which the stove rested. This was a very plausible explanation and was, I believe, accepted, but he was nevertheless ordered to prison for five days – for having caused damage to "royal Prussian property". I was immensely distressed that he should be punished, for I too had done a part of the work, but it was as well that we should not be too closely associated together in the minds of the Germans. Baschwitz left for prison that afternoon, and I was obliged to hide our things under some rubbish in my room. They would certainly have been found here had a search taken place, but the bold Russians had apparently changed their minds, or perhaps the stock of wine at the canteen had given out! I had scarcely hidden the things when I received a message to the effect that the Commandant wished to see me outside. I found him with two other officers of the camp staff, one of whom spoke most excellent English. They wished to know, it appeared, what I was doing in Baschwitz's room that morning, and why I spent so much time with him. I could not see how this latter question concerned them, but I was certain that they only desired a pretext for getting me locked up too, so replied that we were teaching each other languages. The Commandant grunted, apparently far from satisfied, and as I turned to go, one of the officers cried out sarcastically:

"I *say*, Mr. Hardy, you're a bit of an expert, aren't you?"

"An expert at what?" I asked.

"Oh, lots of things," he replied cryptically, and from then on I always rather dreaded this man with his sly face and his Oxford accent.

Several additions were made to the defences while my companion was in prison, for the Germans were evidently convinced that we had a plan of some sort on foot, though they can have had little idea in which direction our intentions lay. Before Baschwitz returned to the camp I had conceived an idea which, though foolish in itself, led us at last on to the right track. I was waiting there to meet him the moment he had passed through the guardroom, and we went straight up to his room. He was ravenous for a cigarette, for he had not been allowed to smoke during his five days, and as soon as he had lighted up I started off and told him my idea.

"Suppose," I said, "that the Germans were to close that latrine and forbid its use, then all we should need to do would be to go down into the courtyard dressed as orderlies, at a time when several of the latter are waiting there, choose a moment when the sentry has his back turned and then jump over into the latrine (for it had no roof). Then we could work undisturbed for any length of time – but we should, of course, have to break out before dark, because those dogs would most certainly spot us when they came with the rounds. We should also need to do it on a rainy day, on account of the sentry outside."

Baschwitz agreed most heartily with all this, but how, said he, were we going to induce the Germans to close the latrine up? My first suggestion was that we should write an anonymous letter to the Commandant, purporting to come from a prisoner, and stating that an attempt to escape was going to be made at that point. He might possibly believe that some man had been actuated by motives of spite – but no, the idea was idiotic when I came to consider it. I was almost ashamed of my suggestion, when suddenly we conceived a most brilliant idea. It might not succeed, but as things stood at the moment it could not possibly do any harm. Baschwitz insisted on taking on himself the harder part, and my role was simply to watch from the window and see exactly what happened. This is what I saw.

Down in the courtyard below me as I stood at the window there were only one or two orderlies washing clothes, and the sentry was walking idly about. At a moment when his back was turned Baschwitz, who had gone downstairs, slipped out of the door and across the yard into the latrine. Had any German been there at the time he would in all probability have been arrested, but by a great stroke of luck the place was empty. He wore an orderly's jacket and cap, but his breeches, putties and boots were obviously those of an officer, which discrepancy had of course been deliberately planned. The moment the sentry had turned and had a clear view of the space between the latrine and the door I raised my hand to my face, which was the prearranged signal, and Baschwitz, keeping his face averted, hurried across to the door and ran quickly upstairs to his room, where he immediately changed into trousers. The sentry had of course, as we had intended, noticed him, though he had not had the time to stop him. He had also observed the very faulty disguise, which was a part of our plan, and I could see that he was uneasy. He went up to one of the orderlies and asked him if that was not an officer who had just left the latrine. The orderly, thinking to help us, shook his head, but the sentry, after hesitating for a moment or two, blew his whistle. In a remarkably short space of time he was joined by the corporal of the guard, and the whole story was rapidly recited. They went off together to examine the latrine and, finding nothing, the corporal made his way to the orderly room. I then left my post of vantage and went back to my room. We expected that the Germans would hold a parade at once in order to give the opportunity to the sentry of identifying Baschwitz, and it was to prevent his being able to do so that Baschwitz had kept his face averted and had afterwards changed his clothes.

No parade was, however, ordered, but about six o'clock that evening, I saw, to my joy, the Commandant and his staff inspecting the latrine. Our whole object in doing what we had done was to make them believe that a reconnaissance had been made of the place, pending a break out. Once convinced of this they were practically certain to do one of two things – either pull the place down, or else close it for everybody. Should they choose the former, we were done. Should they, however, decide on the latter, the problem was almost solved for us.

The following morning, having overslept myself, I was late for roll call, so found myself sentenced to three days' imprisonment. This was most exasperating, but there was nothing to be done, so I had to resign myself to it. The cell in which I spent those three days measured four feet by twelve. The bed was on hinges and during the day was folded and locked up against the wall. I was immensely irritated at finding myself in prison for such a trivial offence, and my impatience to know exactly what had happened in our affair did not make things easier for me. I could have welcomed the escort with open arms when they arrived to march me back.

I felt quite like a free man again as we went through the town, and the delighted smile with which Baschwitz greeted me as I entered the camp was the best news I had had for many a year. Yes, he said, in answer to my whispered question; they had closed it, the poor benighted idiots! A plank had been nailed across the door and otherwise no changes had been made. Oh, what a relief! For once in a while they had played into our hands, and now, for Heaven's sake, a cigarette!

Chapter Nine

Everything was ready. We had arranged about civilian clothes for each of us; we had between us about a hundred and twenty marks in German money, a compass and the small map out of a railway timetable. We each had a pocket knife, and a small store of food which we intended to carry in our pockets, and the small saw was hidden till we should need it. All that remained to us to do now was to perfect the plan of our movements once outside the camp, and then to await a rainy day.

We had heard by now, directly and indirectly, of a certain number of attempts to escape, and from everybody possessed of any knowledge whatever on the subject we had heard evil reports of the frontiers, both of Holland and Switzerland. The Danish frontier did not come much into the calculations of prisoners, for to get there one had necessarily to cross the Kiel Canal, and this was probably the most strictly guarded district in Germany. I had already had experience of the Baltic coast and indeed had been very near to success there. I had never forgotten the words of a German soldier in the cell next to mine at Stralsund. On hearing the details of the affair, he had told me that it was a great mistake to have tried to get on a boat at Stralsund, but that I should have taken the steamer to Rügen Island and then tried for a ship at Sassnitz, a port on the northern coast of Rügen. Everything, therefore, seemed to indicate the advisability of making another attempt in this direction, and eventually we decided upon it. We could not, we thought, travel together in the train. We were quite independent of each other, and it would be much safer if we kept to separate compartments.

Baschwitz, as I have said, had lived several years in Africa, and here also were all his brother's interests. It appeared that a certain rich and influential German had had many business dealings with this brother, whom he knew well. He was now, it was believed, employed at the German Foreign Office, and had written to Baschwitz, whom he had met once or twice during the War. Our idea was that we should visit this man and ask him if he would give us any help. It seemed a very dangerous undertaking, but all escape was dangerous, and should we succeed in gaining this man's assistance it would mean our freedom. So we decided to travel to Stralsund via Berlin, in a suburb of which this German lived.

The weather at this time was remarkably fine and we were hard put to it to pass our time away. All day long we used to lie outside in the sun and watch the others playing tennis. Baschwitz was a most delightful conversationalist, and for hours on end I used to listen to his adventures. We spent a large part of the time planning what we would do if we got home, but we were both very superstitious and never spoke of this with any certainty. We had secret jokes about many of the other prisoners and used to get the greatest amusement out of them. I am afraid we used to feel ourselves very superior in asmuch as we were trying to get away, and used not to enter into the life of the camp at all. My own countrymen were very sporting here. White flannels from home were much in vogue and the cinder court was never free. Their efforts were immensely admired by a band of young Belgian officers, who became in time more English than we were ourselves! They were never to be seen without pipes in their mouths, and it was quite useless to try to talk French to them, for they invariably answered in our own language, and they even used it among themselves. I am afraid Baschwitz and I were not very popular here. Our loud guffaws at the efforts of these people to amuse themselves had, I fear, something nasty about them, but somehow I felt inclined to wear my very oldest clothes, talk Cockney and give up shaving. The Russians drank and gambled incessantly. One of them (I think he must have been the first of all Bolsheviks) had recently returned from prison, to which he had been sentenced for three months for stabbing and killing a friend! The other Russians had prepared to give him a cold reception on his return, but on his announcing that if any of his countrymen cut him, or showed any inclination to avoid him, he would do a few more murders, he became the most sought after person in the camp. Most people appeared to think that we had given up any idea which we had previously entertained, and we were often asked laughingly whether we were going to escape or not; but one had to learn to take these jokes in good part.

I need not say that we were all this time very anxious. The slightest change in routine made by the Germans might throw all our plans out, but we could do nothing. The usual rumours of amazingly plucky attempts just about to be made by a determined gang of Russians came to terrify us, but always the leader became sober at the critical moment, or else the treasurer became drunk and lost all the gang's money at the roulette-table! A system of walks on parole had just been established, but Baschwitz and I did not feel that we were justified in taking part in them, and we were also convinced that, should we escape and be retaken, the Germans would accuse us of having gleaned information while outside the camp on parole. We were up by six o'clock every morning at this time, for it was essential to us to know early if a wet day was probable; but weeks passed and there was still no sign of rain.

We had completed our arrangements for faking both evening and morning roll calls for at least three days after our break out. Baschwitz had one night placed his dummy in bed and had then hidden himself behind a screen during roll call. The Germans had passed it without hesitation, and this shows how perfect had been his workmanship. In my own room, on the other hand, this trick would never succeed. One solution was to make a second dummy and substitute it for another officer out of Baschwitz's room, who, in turn, would replace me in mine after I had gone. But there was no more plaster to be had, and I sadly feared that I was up against an impossibility, until one night I noticed a thing which solved the whole difficulty for me. I should have explained that these roll calls, properly speaking, were merely a process of identification, or intended to be such, and involved no answering to one's name. The officer in charge of my room took, as I have said, the greatest care to satisfy himself that the occupant of each bed was a real live man. For three nights running I watched him while he made his round of the room, and I came to the conclusion that neither he nor the sentries with him did more than this. *They did not count the beds,* and all I had to do was to take my bed to pieces before we left, conceal the sections and then move the others along to hide the gap.

Morning roll call had been much more difficult to manage, but we had now arranged with two Belgian officers that they should help us. One of them lived in Baschwitz's room, the other in mine, and they both appeared to be extraordinarily decent fellows. They had nothing whatever to gain by it, and helped us out of the goodness of their hearts, and it is with the deepest regret that I have to record that both of them were eventually punished for their part in the affair. The plan was that, the morning after we had gone, they should report themselves sick and unable to attend roll call outside. They would, however, appear on parade, but standing well back to avoid any chance of recognition. The Germans, owing to our absence, would report two officers missing, and would then be reminded that there were two sick upstairs. Roll call being declared finished, the officer in charge would go up to the rooms to make sure that all was correct, and would find the two Belgians in bed, for they could, by entering the building through another door, just beat him by a short head. It was a very old trick to hide the absence of one prisoner by inducing the Germans unconsciously to count another man twice.

And then at last the day came, for I got up early one morning to find it raining heavily out of a grey sky. God knows if I was altogether glad. One had grown so used to looking into the future, and so accustomed to the feeling that one was *going* to escape, that one felt qualms when faced with the necessity of putting one's scheme to the test. I have known men to work for months at a time digging a tunnel under the most difficult circumstances; many became ill, but worked on; many, in spite of festering sores on knees and elbows, continued to spend five hours a day crawling about underground; all were exhausted by lack of air before the day's work was over; and yet, when the task was finished, one found a number of these men had made no preparations for their escape, and could not even nerve themselves up to take advantage of the opportunity. All this is very curious and difficult to understand, but in my opinion it does undoubtedly require a great mental effort to drive oneself on to take the plunge in these most unpleasant affairs. We had very clearly recognized, and had often discussed, the probability of one or other of us being shot while making this attempt. All sentries in this corps had instructions to fire without warning in the event of a break out, and we expected short shrift if we were seen. I was never one of those lucky people who do not suffer from terror of sudden death or sudden mutilation, and I think that Baschwitz too knew well the meaning of fear, though a braver man I shall never meet.

He was awake and shaving when I went into his room. As he turned towards me I saw that he had cut his moustache down to a few ragged bristles, and I immediately assumed my limp and my "dud" eye. He laughed and, looking at me critically, said:

"Oui, c'est justement ça. After the breakfast we go!"

"You bet," said I with a grin and an odd feeling about my middle. "Got everything ready?"

"Alles," he answered, for we always mixed our languages in the most laughable way, and rarely answered each other in the language in which we had been addressed.

I went back to my room and started to get my things ready. I took both our civilian jackets and, wrapping them up as small as I possibly could, gave them to a British orderly with whom it had been previously arranged that he should help us. We had found ourselves unable to wear our Tommies' kit over them and had, therefore, asked this man to carry them down for us and drop them over the wall of the latrine. I watched him anxiously from the window as he crossed the yard, carrying them in such a way as not to be seen by the sentry. He chose his moment well, and, throwing them over, walked back, but the German seemed after all to have noticed that he was empty-handed as he returned, for I saw him walk to the lavatory and attempt to look over the top. Had he been able to do so he would have seen the clothes lying on the ground, but the wall was too high, and he appeared to lose interest in the matter. His subconscious suspicions might, however, have been aroused, though he might hardly know it himself, and we decided that we must wait until he was relieved. Breakfast was a horrible meal to me. The sight of food disgusted me, but I knew that I should be hungry before midday and forced myself to eat. I was awfully nervous, though I did my best to hide it. So much hung in the balance, and it was so impossible to foresee how the affair would end – in complete success or in catastrophe. I got up from the table and fetched a small spanner which I had made out of the handle of a metal spoon.

This was for the use of the Belgian who was going to take my bed to pieces, and I gave it to him. I then went over and said "Goodbye" to the English in my room. Most of them looked at me open mouthed when I told them what was going to happen, but they all wished me the best of luck. The man to whom I had given the cheque asked if he could be of any assistance, and seemed hurt when I told him that everything had been arranged for.

"This," he said, "is anyway the least I can do," and, fetching the cheque, he tore it up before my eyes.

A thing like this made one feel good, and the idea that what one was doing made one worthy of consideration was very welcome.

About this time a great commotion broke out in Baschwitz's room, and I hurried along to find out what had happened. I found my friend quite unlike himself, in a tremendously excited state. It appeared that, finding himself in need of a civilian button, he had asked a Belgian major to give him one off his jacket, and had been refused. This had simply infuriated him, and he was shouting and yelling at the top of his voice, and his language did credit to his military training! I managed to soothe him a little, and he set about completing his preparations, but whenever he caught the eye of the major, who sat sulking in a corner like an obstinate child, he would break into curses again. We were ready before the sentry was relieved, and consequently had another ten minutes to wait. We sat there with a crowd of Baschwitz's countrymen round us, and they had a peculiarly considerate and commiserating air about them, for this is always how one feels towards a prisoner who is just about to "go in off the deep end". What makes *him* feel so bad is the knowledge that it is all *his* fault; that, whatever happens, he is responsible and he is to blame. This is indeed a delightful realization should he succeed but – how often does he succeed?

"Il est parti," said a friend who had been doing duty at the window.

Picking up a piece of raw bacon with which to lubricate the saw, I buttoned up my military greatcoat and followed Baschwitz and his friend downstairs. We stood waiting in the passage, well back from the door, and in this way could watch the sentry and choose our moment without being seen by him. The sentry came out of his box and walked towards the door, and we were both trembling with excitement as we unbuttoned our greatcoats. In spite of our disguise we did not wish him to see us if it could possibly be avoided, and, as he turned to walk back, we flung our coats to the accomplice and hurried out into the yard. There were several orderlies there, and the sentry did not turn at the sound of our footsteps. We reached the latrine and I saw the men looking at us in astonishment as we scrambled over the wall and dropped inside, but they realized at once what was happening, and played up to us in fine style. My hat! what luck! if everything went as well as this first part, we should be free men within a week! And now for the job.

We knelt down and critically examined the planks through which we had to cut. They were very thick, and the little slim saw which I had procured seemed quite inadequate to the work. However, we must do our best, so I lay down on my stomach and began using one of our knives to cut a hole through which the saw could be inserted. We worked in turns for about twenty minutes before this was finished, but found to our consternation that we were making a great deal of noise, and that this could not be avoided, however much grease was used. We should have to cut through two planks at a distance of about eighteen inches from the ground, but it was becoming clear to us that we should never be able to finish this without being overheard, for it must be remembered that neither the sentry in the courtyard nor the man on the embankment was more than ten yards from us. Our second shock was the discovery that where we lay we were in full view of the parcels office window. There were always several Germans in this office, which was at the top of the building, and we thought it very probable that we had already been seen. We could not, we said to each other, expect everybody to be blind, and there was a very good chance that the sentry outside would notice the end of our saw. The rain had completely stopped, and we began to realize what an absurdly difficult enterprise we had undertaken. However, there was nothing to be done but push on with the work, though we would not have given much for our chances of success as things were now. I took off my orderly's clothes and then relieved Baschwitz at his sawing while he did the same. At last the two planks had been cut through, but the wood being wet we had some difficulty in getting them out. We first screwed across them, to hold them together, a piece of wood which we had brought for the purpose, and then, as we prised with our knives, the piece suddenly came away. We replaced it at once, buried the saw and other things that we did not want, closed our knives and put them in our pockets, and then prepared for the worst part of all.

I was to go first, but my position was enviable compared with Baschwitz's, for he would have to replace the plank from outside. I pushed it through, and then, with one arm, extended above my head and the other close by my side, I managed after one furious struggle to get through. The first thing I saw was the sentry, but he was standing outside his box with his back towards us and was watching something with great interest in the direction of the river bank. I turned to my left, and crawled up the ditch formed by the paling on one side and the embankment on the other. A few yards ahead of me the ground rose to a level with the railway line, so that beyond this point we should have no means of concealing ourselves. Baschwitz had experienced a certain amount of difficulty in replacing the board, and it must indeed have been a horrible moment for him as he struggled with it. At any moment it might slip and fall with a thud; at any moment the sentry might turn of his own accord, might actually have turned and be aiming now —! But my friend never so much as glanced over his shoulder till he had finished it to his satisfaction. He picked up a handful of mud and rubbed it over the new cut and then crawled slowly towards me, and I patted him on the back, at which he grinned. We reached the point where the ground rose, and having satisfied ourselves that the sentry was not looking in our direction, stood up and – found confronting us, not two yards away, another sentry in charge of some French prisoners working on the line! This man had nothing whatever to do with the camp, but he stared in astonishment at seeing us rise suddenly out of the earth. For one weak moment I felt inclined to duck, but to show that we feared him would have been fatal. I turned, therefore, to Baschwitz and said in German: "But where can he be? If we've lost that dog there'll be trouble."

"Dass ist ja wahr," he said.

Whistling and peering in all directions, we crossed the line and slid down the embankment on the other side. The camp sentry looked very surprised. No civilian was allowed here, and we had constantly seen even railway officials stopped and questioned. It was obvious that he could not understand how we had got there without his seeing us, but he evidently believed that the other sentry had satisfied himself as to our *bona fides* and had authorized us to pass. We reached the river bank and turned upstream, knowing that from here we could get easily into the town. We scarcely dared to look to right or left, but spoke to each other in German for the benefit of anyone who might pass us. I was glad – my faith, but I was glad, and grateful too, for such luck as we had had comes seldom in a lifetime. As for Baschwitz, this was the first time he had ever succeeded in getting clear of a camp, and he was beside himself. He took me by the arm and squeezed it, "Honours easy," he said under his breath, and then aloud:

"Ich kann es nicht glauben, ich kann es nicht glauben!"

Chapter Ten

As we walked through the town towards the station we could think of nothing but the wonderful way fortune had favoured us. We *must* succeed now, we thought. No one had ever had a better chance, for our escape was unknown in the camp, and we had many hours' start. It was eleven o'clock before we reached the station and we had only just time to get our tickets (at separate booking offices) before the train came in. I got into a non-smoking compartment, for I always did my best to avoid soldiers, but Baschwitz spoke such perfect German, and was such an accomplished liar, that it was a matter of indifference to him with whom he travelled. Our journey was quite an uneventful one, and we had not even to change. Most of my fellow passengers were women, and as I pretended to sleep most of the time no one spoke to me. It was a delightful sensation to feel oneself being carried each minute a little further from the scene of one's late troubles, and to know that on leaving the train one would not have to face all those other difficulties alone. We reached Berlin about 12.30, and walked out into the busy streets. The weather had completely changed since early morning, and everything was bathed in bright sunshine. We approached the nearest policeman, as we had arranged to do when necessary, and learnt from him the best way to our destination. We then set off for the tramway centre, and on the way passed the school where Baschwitz had been as a child. We were very gay, and had been much amused by the fact that the policeman, while pointing out the direction to us, had put his hand on my companion's shoulder. A tram was just moving off as we approached the centre and Baschwitz, running ahead, jumped on board and asked the conductress if it went to Charlottenburg. On her replying that it did he signalled me to hurry, but I dared not break into a run, for I had been limping so markedly that I could not possibly have escaped notice. Very lame men do not run after trams and a blunder of this kind on my part might have given us both away, so I was obliged to disappear. There were many people on the steps of the tram below him, and I thought it might be some time before he succeeded in getting off, but I had not gone far before I saw him running towards me, and this time we made sure of getting on together. We had a short walk after leaving the tram and had to make several inquiries before we found the house we were looking for. We had arranged for Baschwitz to call here alone, and for me to walk about until he could let me know the result of his visit. It would not, of course, do to wait outside, as the Berlin police are very inquisitive, and I looked none too respectable in my shabby civilian clothes. On returning to the house I found him waiting for me, and as we walked away he told me what had happened.

A maid had, it appeared, opened the door, but the mistress of the house was standing in the hall, and, hearing her husband's name mentioned, had come forward. Baschwitz had met this lady several times before the War, and was never able to say with certainty that she did not recognize him. There is a peculiar depth and subtlety about many Germans, and they do not by any means always do the obvious thing. She told him that her husband had gone to Constantinople and would not be back for several months, but that she herself could transact any business that my friend might have with him. This was very disconcerting, and she smiled when he replied that he had a letter which he was only to deliver personally. Instead of asking to see it she questioned him as to why he was not in uniform. He said he had been lately invalided out of the Army, and at this she had looked at him queerly for a long time and had then fetched a handful of her husband's cigars, which she gave to him before he took his leave. He had not an easy face to forget, Baschwitz, and I often wonder how much this fashionable young Berlin lady knew!

We decided now, in order to fill up the time, to walk the whole way to the Stettiner Bahnhof, and this we did, arriving there about four o'clock in the afternoon. Our train did not leave till half past five, so we bought our tickets (for it is always as well to have something to show if questioned), and then were faced with the necessity of tramping the streets for another hour. All this was rather unsatisfactory, for it became very exhausting, but my experience of waiting-rooms was not such as to encourage me to take advantage of them. We were back

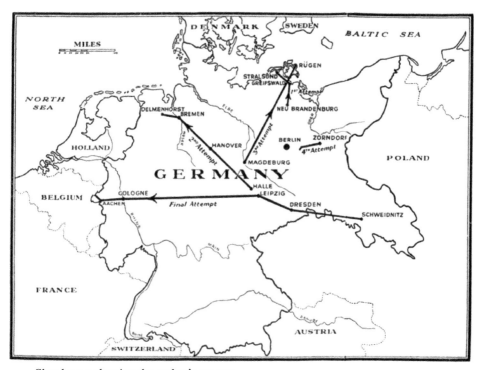

Sketch map showing the author's escapes.

in good time for the train, and, as before, separated and travelled in different compartments. I was alone practically the whole journey, but Baschwitz, I believe, was talking to different people most of the time. We ran into Stralsund at midnight, and it brought most vividly back to my mind the events of the year before as we walked through the streets of the silent town. All very old and very beautiful – steep cobbled streets, and high, weather-beaten walls, and no one to be seen but an occasional Schützmann on his beat.

With my knowledge of the place I was able to lead my companion clear of it before long, and in a field about two miles outside, along the Greifswald Road, we decided to spend the night. Our legs ached so much after our unaccustomed exercise that we were obliged to lie on our backs and hold them in the air! We ate a small part of our food, smoked interminable cigarettes and talked until dawn, for neither of us was able to sleep. About six o'clock, feeling very dirty and unkempt after our night out, we started back to the town, and reached the harbour about half past six. I was surprised to see that there was scarcely a single ship in port, which boded badly for our enterprise. Things were apparently much changed since the previous year, but we persuaded each other that they would wear a more encouraging face at Sassnitz. To cross over to Rügen, one buys a ticket at a small station on the quay; the train runs on board the steamer, and runs ashore again on the other side, and across the island. We thought it very probable that we should be asked for papers, but this did not occur, and we were able to get into the train without hindrance. It was very interesting to see how the whole affair was worked, as I had not previously seen this type of ferry.

The crossing took about twenty minutes, and, being in adjacent compartments, we were able to lean out of the window and talk to each other. As soon as we reached Rügen a number of people boarded the train, and we observed, much to our consternation, that they spoke a *patois* of their own, which was as unintelligible to Baschwitz as it was to me.

Sassnitz is built practically up and down the face of a cliff. It is a town of white houses and red roofs, of precipitous cobbled streets and quaint little shops – and to be there on that bright summer morning was almost to be in England again! Away below us as we descended through the town lay the harbour with its long mole, and the blue sea, while far away on the horizon, seen faintly as a dim cloud, lay the coast of Sweden. We thought it wise to buy some food if possible, for we had very little left. Several shops had chocolate for sale, but we had not the appearance of people who could afford such luxuries, so we decided against getting any. Later on, however, we had a bright idea; Baschwitz went into a shop, and pulling a slip of paper out of his pocket glanced at it and said:

"I am to order five marks' worth of chocolate, a pound of apples and two pounds of biscuits."

The things were naturally sold to him without question, and meanwhile I had entered another shop and bought a little cheese and some jam. The latter was given to me on a piece of newspaper, and carrying this awkward parcel in my hand I rejoined my friend in the street. Our consternation on reaching the harbour and finding not one single ship in port can well be imagined. The harbour was altogether smaller than I had expected and no work was going on there of any kind. We looked at each other speechlessly, beginning to realize that we had made a very serious blunder in coming here at all. We turned away and walked along the beach until we were clear of the town.

It was quite useless to start commiserating with ourselves; the only thing to do was to eat our food, have a rest, and decide how we could best readjust our plans to meet this very unexpected misfortune. We found a spot among some rocks where there was little chance of our being noticed, and here we sat down and ate our meal and discussed our next move.

The quay was deserted but for a couple of sentries, who stood at the barriers, and there were apparently no legitimate passengers waiting to cross. Ships still ran from Sassnitz to Trelleborg, that we knew, but what chance had we of stowing away with circumstances as they were? We had not seen even so much as a fishing smack yet, but we had heard that Arcona, a village about fifteen miles further up the coast, was still a busy fishing port. We therefore eventually decided to push on to this point, and – if we failed in our efforts to bribe some fisherman to help us – to cross the island again and return to the mainland. We might find getting off the island not quite so easy as getting on! but should we succeed, we would then make for the Dutch frontier. This would necessitate another two days' railway travelling, but we thought we should have just enough money if we were careful. Having come to this decision, we lay down for a sleep.

It was four o'clock in the afternoon when I woke up to find my companion gone. A steamer was moored alongside the mole, and I knew that he must have gone to investigate. Within half an hour he returned, shaking his head. No, there was nothing to be done. No one had gone on board or come ashore, and the barrier had not even been raised. She was, he thought, a Swedish mail boat and probably carried letters and parcels for Russian prisoners. Satisfied that we were leaving no chances behind us, we packed up what remained of our food – abandoning the jam, into which the ants had found their way – and set off for Arcona. We followed a track which led for mile after mile through woods on the edge of the cliff. Here and there the cliff rose to a great height, and at such points of vantage we would spy a sentry gazing out to sea. Once or twice these fellows passed us on the way to their posts and, though some of them looked at us curiously, we were not challenged. About eight o'clock in the evening, as we passed through a small village, we noticed a group of men who appeared to scrutinize us unpleasantly. We heard afterwards that two Russian prisoners had escaped from a camp on the island and at this time had not yet been captured, and it was doubtless for these two that people were on the qui vive. I glanced back and saw that after a little hesitation they were following us. I whispered to Baschwitz and we at once swung round and walked back towards them, calling out to know if they could tell us of a place where we could spend the night. They grinned sheepishly at each other on hearing Baschwitz's colloquial German, and told us in quite a friendly way that we should probably be able to get a night's lodging at the house of Widow Schröder who, it appeared, kept a small inn on the outskirts of the next village. We thanked them and, as we pushed on, I heard them laughing among themselves, but we could not understand their sudden suspicion of us. It had begun to rain and had turned fairly cold before we reached the house we looked for, and it was with great relief that we found it, for the prospect of a night in the rain was not alluring.

We entered the little bar-parlour, which appeared empty but for the old woman behind the bar, and asked whether she could let us have two beds for the night. No! in a shrill ill-tempered voice – she wouldn't! Her house was full and anyway she was very particular who she received as guests. She didn't like the looks of us, and perhaps the under-officer would like to see our papers!

What under-officer? We started to bluster and protest, but the thrice-accursed old hag had done the mischief, for a man got up from a chair and came forward into the light – a N.C.O. of Landsturm with a red beard and foxy eyes.

"Yes," he said, "let me have a look at your papers," and as he spoke he opened the door and called two of his men, who came at once into the room.

By God! we were trapped! The place was a guardroom full of soldiers and – the game was up!

And then, quietly and fluently, without a trace of nervousness, this splendid pal of mine started to lie!

We had arranged no story and, paralysed though I was by the sudden turn of affairs, I was interested to hear his yarn. We were cousins, it appeared, and he had been invalided out of the Army before the War on account of fever which he had caught in East Africa; I was unfit for service on account of my eye, and we had been employed together in a factory at Stettin. Our people were, however, in Sweden, and we had just received from the police the necessary passes to enable us to join them there. The passports had been taken from us at Sassnitz that morning, as there were certain papers requiring verification. It was amusing, he said, that on our last night in Germany we should be arrested. This explanation set everybody thinking hard. Many soldiers had by now entered the room, and they on the whole appeared to be on our side. On the other hand the old woman and her two loathsome daughters were horribly suspicious. One of them spoke to us in a dialect which was scarcely recognizable as German, and then when we failed to understand shouted triumphantly:

"Ha, you say you are from Stettin, but so becomes it in Stettin spoken, and you understand not!"

We hastened to explain that we were Berliners by birth, but this point had told against us. The under-officer ordered that we should be led into the next room, which was the guardroom, and himself went out in order to telephone to the Sassnitz police.

We found ourselves in a low-ceiled kitchen with tiled floors. Four soldiers sat playing cards at a table and several others lolled about the room. Half a dozen rifles stood in an improvised rack, equipment lay everywhere; on a shelf a few loaves of war bread; many old and dirty newspapers in one corner – the usual paraphernalia of a German guardroom. They all stared curiously at us as we were brought in, but I had no eyes for them. Hanging on the wall immediately opposite me as I entered was a typically hideously ornamented card with a text printed on it. It was fly-specked and faded, but the words that it bore seemed to come to me as a message: "Wer im Gott vertraut, der kann alles thun" ("He who trusts in God will find all things possible").

I edged nearer to Baschwitz, and whispered to him in German: "We shall get out of this!"

He shook his head miserably and signalled to me to keep silence, for many eyes were upon us. Another N.C.O. now sat down at the table with a pen in his hand, and began taking particulars from us. We were not searched, for they were by no means certain that our story was untrue, but many very difficult questions were put to us, and it was only by the merest luck that we were not identified as foreigners. In the middle of this cross examination the under-officer returned from the telephone office and said it was too late to get through to Sassnitz, and that we should have to spend the night in the guardroom. We were to consider ourselves under arrest, and in the morning they would find out all right who we were, and he laughed meaningly. Baschwitz suggested that we should be allowed to sleep, and he indicated to us a couple of iron bedsteads in a corner, over which a single mattress had been thrown corner-wise. We walked over and, taking our boots off, lay down and the Unteroffizier followed us with a lamp. This he placed on a table near us, and then signalled to two men to pick up their rifles and sit within reach of us.

This they did in silence and I heard them load with scarcely a sound, and then, having placed their chairs in such a way as to hem us in, they sat down for their long vigil.

"Wer im Gott vertraut" – ja, aber, could anything have looked more perfectly hopeless? A dash from the room was impossible, for there were several men in addition to the sentries between us and the door. Here we should inevitably have to remain till the morning – here we should be when the under-officer returned from telephoning with the information that the police repudiated all knowledge of us, and that our whole story was a lie; and from that moment we were lost, for we should be conveyed to prison and held in custody until we declared ourselves prisoners of war. Nevertheless, I thought it best that we should destroy anything likely to serve as a clue to the Germans, and I whispered to Baschwitz to hand me the photograph of himself in uniform which he carried. He did so without a question, and I tore it to fragments and pushed them well under a closet which stood near the bed. I opened my own shirt and bit through the string of my identity disc, which latter I pushed down into my boot. It all seemed very futile, but the thought of that text never left me. It had come at a moment when I had lost all hope … it *must* mean something. Perhaps … and with these thoughts I fell asleep.

Chapter Eleven

I t was daylight before I opened my eyes and glanced at my watch. It was ten minutes to five. For a few minutes I lay there still scarcely awake, and slowly the details of yesterday's catastrophe passed through my mind. I was stiff and sore and utterly dejected, realizing that this must indeed be the last chance I should ever have, nor could I conceive what had induced us to make the unpardonable blunder of entering this place at all. Better a month in the rain, better have died of exposure than that this should be the end.

I sat up on the bed, and suddenly my jaw dropped and I stared with wide open eyes. The scene which met my gaze was certainly enough to account for my astonishment. The sentries were still seated side by side in their chairs and leaning over their rifles, while on the sofa lay the under-officer with a handkerchief over his face. All three were sound asleep and there were no other soldiers in the room. I got up on the bed and swore softly as it creaked. I had to pass between the sentries to reach the window, but I was in my stocking-feet and I made not a sound. The window was jammed tight and it was clear to me that I should not be able to open it without considerable noise, so I moved over to the door with a hurried glance round to see if any wire lay about. I found a piece which had been used to hold a picture, and having rapidly prepared two instruments I knelt before the keyhole, only to discover immediately that all my work had been unnecessary, for the door was unlocked! I crept back to the bed and woke Baschwitz, putting my hand over his mouth to prevent his making a sound. I pointed to the sleeping sentries and made a little gesture of invitation towards the door. As I dragged on my boots I looked again at my watch, and realized that we had only three minutes before the old guard would return, for the relief must have already left. "Vite! vite! vite!" I whispered to my friend, who was pulling furiously at his boots with a look of excitement and joy on his face that was a pleasure to behold. "Je vous crois!" he replied, and seeing that he was almost ready, I passed between the sentries scarcely daring to put foot to the ground – reached the door and stood once more in the fresh air, a free man.

Baschwitz joined me a moment later, and keeping to the edge of the road where the sand lay thick, we broke into a jog-trot. He thumped me on the back as we ran saying, "Mon ami, je suis content de vous," and I laughed. I – well, I was content with the whole world, and felt that God had worked a miracle for us. We ran for about a mile without stopping and then, seeing a forest in front of us, decided to leave the road and keep in among the trees. We were going northwards and this may possibly have been a mistake, but it did not really much matter which direction we took, for the alarm would certainly be out by now and our way to the mainland barred. It appeared that our best alternative would now be to make for the other side of the island, try to steal a small boat and sail into Stralsund harbour that night. Our first object, however, must be to get well clear of the scene of our recent experiences, for we feared that dogs would be employed to track us down.

For three hours we walked and ran without ceasing, and then, feeling that we could go no further, lay down for a short rest. In ten minutes we were up and off again, and striking a road followed it clear of the woods and on to the heath, but we saw other woods a few miles ahead of us and pushed on. We had not been long on the road when a civilian passed us on a bicycle. He bade us good day and did not look round at us, but on reaching a small group of houses we found he had dismounted and was waiting there. As we passed he shouted out:

"Ein Augenblick. Ich möchte gern wissen woher Sie kommen." We stopped and then walked up to him, and as we did so I saw a frightened look in his eye and he glanced round as though looking for help. Neither of us looked very gentlemanly, and Baschwitz's voice was far from pleasant as he asked the man what he had said. He had asked us where we came from, but now all he could say was:

"Ja, ich muss nämlich aufpassen" ("I have to watch out").

"Yes," said Baschwitz, looking positively devilish, "you have to watch out!" and we turned with a laugh and walked on. I looked round and saw the man leap once more on to his bicycle and ride towards a house from which telegraph wires ran. Oh, for a pair of climbing-irons and some wire-cutters, I thought! We could still have forestalled him, but without these we were helpless, although we knew that the very wires over our heads were carrying the news of our whereabouts. Again we broke into a run, and at last, thoroughly done, we reached the woods to our front, only to find them scarcely more than a big copse. On our way we had passed a group of boys, who had taken to their heels on seeing us, but we knew that they would give information as to where we had hidden ourselves and that the game was up. We found a small ditch in the copse into which we fell panting, but it was clear that, with the numbers they would have against us, they would beat every bush until we were discovered.

About twenty minutes later I saw the first of our pursuers. I climbed a small tree and from here could see several soldiers with their rifles at the trail moving towards us, while from another direction came other soldiers and a few civilians with shotguns. I climbed down and told Baschwitz how things stood, and he laughed and, pulling out his case, offered me a cigarette. We lit up, and then with one accord linked arms and walked towards the edge of the wood. We should indeed be lucky if there were no firing, but if we had to stop one, we felt it was better, here in the open, than tangled in the wire of a prisoners' camp.

As we emerged from the woods, not a word was spoken, but we found ourselves covered by ten or twelve rifles. We halted, and nervous though I was, I took another pull at my cigarette, and then, throwing it away from me, called out: "All right, we're done." A soldier walked up to me and placed the muzzle of his rifle against my chest and, "Yes," he said, "you're done, you bloody murderer!"

I did not at the time altogether understand this remark. It was customary among the Germans to speak of their own dead as having been murdered, while those of the Entente had been killed by the gallant Feldgrau defending his Fatherland, and we were, therefore, accustomed to hearing ourselves called hired assassins. But it surprised me that he should use this term before it had even been ascertained that we were prisoners of war, and the fury and threats of the crowd convinced me that some incident had occurred of which we knew nothing. Things looked in fact so black that we thought it as well to mention that we were officers, for the word always carries a certain amount of weight with it in Germany. We had much difficulty in making them believe this, but eventually they seemed to accept the statement and, an escort having been organized, we were marched off to Alt Kirchen, the nearest village. We had sworn to each other that we would not put up our hands under any circumstances, and it was a relief to both of us that we had not been called upon to do so. On reaching the village a police inspector was fetched, and this man, dismissing the escort with the exception of two sentries, conducted us in front of the local magistrate.

This latter proved to be a very fierce old man, who took down the depositions in the minutest detail, and then ordered that we should be locked up in the gaol and the Stralsund police communicated with. We were accordingly marched away, and locked together in a small and filthy cell. I should imagine that this place had not been cleaned within the memory of man, and it abounded in lice and fleas. We were hungry, so hungry in fact that it became our principal idea, and made us almost forget the disaster that had befallen us. We took it in turns to beat on the door and howl for food, but to no avail; and we even pretended to commit suicide in the hope of attracting the attention of the Germans. Suspended by our necks apparently from the bars of the window – heads at an angle and tongues protruding – we must indeed have presented a pleasant spectacle! but no one paid the slightest attention to us, and we were fain to lie down and try to sleep. This was, however, impossible on account of the bugs, and before long, already bitten in innumerable places, we started up and began to walk up and down the cell. It was eight o'clock that evening before any food was brought to us, and by then we were famished. We each got a bowl of stew and a slice of bread, which made, I think, the most welcome meal I ever sat down to. We spent a miserable night and found ourselves, in spite of all our efforts to prevent it, a mass of bites in the morning. About six o'clock we were given some coffee and a few slices of bread, but we had of course nothing to smoke, which was a greater hardship to Baschwitz even than to myself. It was the greatest relief to us to hear about midday that the guard had arrived to take us to the mainland. It consisted of six men and a Feldwebel, which struck me at the time as a very strong escort for two prisoners. We were ordered by the Feldwebel to clean out the cell before leaving, and on our refusing two of the sentries were ordered to prepare to fire. We were, however, determined not to suffer this humiliation, and were convinced that the Feldwebel would not dare to order us to be shot on such a trivial affair, though the sentries appeared to think he meant business and, contrary to the popular conception of the bloodthirsty German soldier, looked horribly white and terrified. The effect of a few minutes' bellowing was tried, but we also both could, and did, bellow in fine style, with the result that the attempt at coercing us was abandoned. We should be reported, yes, for disobeying orders, yes! we should be am strengsten bestraft, ja! Na, warten Sie mal, Sie werden bald was lernen!" *Marsch!*"

On arriving at Bergen, the capital of the island, we had to change trains, and the threats and yells of the people who crowded round us gave us to understand that in some inexplicable way the rumour had got about that we had been arrested for murdering some one or other. This explained the remark of the sentry when first we had been taken, but we were at a loss to understand how such an idea had arisen. An N.C.O., simply foaming with rage, reached the door of the carriage and began abusing the guards for their hesitation before shooting a couple of murderers. He was pushed off the footboard by the Feldwebel in charge, who remarked: "The case is not yet proved!" The case not yet *proved?* My hat! things were beginning to look pretty serious, I thought.

On our arrival at Stralsund we were marched through the town to that same prison where I had spent a night with Wasilief the previous year. We found a most objectionable fellow in charge—a Feldwebel. We were locked in separate cells, and were told that we should be allowed no communication with each other, being "Untersuchungschaft-Gefangenen", but that we should be permitted to have our meals brought from a neighbouring hotel at a cost of six marks a day. This, of course, would be taken from the money in our possession. The Feldwebel had a most insolent manner of unlocking my cell door at odd moments of the day in order to tell me a few more details of what England's fate would be once she became German. He did not find me a very satisfactory subject for his humour, and grew to hate me like poison, though to Baschwitz he was, I believe, slightly more civil. He even told him that he had intended to allow him to smoke, but that on his mentioning this fact to me I had said that I would inform against him. All Englishmen, Baschwitz was to understand, were traitors by nature – he knew them. The day after our arrival in the prison I was sent for to appear before the Gerichts Offizier for the purpose of having my statement taken down. I found him a horrible, white faced, cropped-headed creature with a thick neck and pale eyes distorted by his strong glasses. He was incredibly haughty and refused to address a single word to me, though God knows I had no desire for any conversation with him. Every question was put to me through an interpreter, who, however, finding that I knew considerably more German than he did English, merely repeated the words to me. I was just about to leave the room, having signed my statement, when I heard the interpreter instructed to ask me what I knew concerning the death of the under-officer who had arrested us in the inn. I replied that I knew nothing whatever of the event, though the question explained to me much that I had not understood. It was some time, however, before we learned the real facts of the case, and I now understand the Germans' wish to keep us in ignorance of them, for we undoubtedly derived a certain amount of satisfaction from them. It appeared that within five minutes of our escaping from the inn the under-officer had awakened to find us gone. Without a word to anyone he had pulled off his boot, and then, toe on trigger, with the muzzle of his rifle in his mouth, had blown his brains out. One cannot but admire a man who chooses death rather than to live with the knowledge that he has failed in his duty. For that wretched old woman it was, however, let us hope, a fitting lesson. By her interference and her lack of sympathy with two poor strangers against whom she knew nothing, she had brought about the whole affair. Incidentally she had caused our undoing, and I still feel a most uncompromising hatred for her.

For five days we were kept at Stralsund; until, I presume, the inquest had been held, and we had been exonerated from blame. During that time we were allowed one hour's exercise daily in the prison yard, but not of course together, and beyond this had to pass the time as best we could in our cells. With no one to speak to, nothing to read and nothing to smoke, with the prospect of many months' confinement before us, and the memory of our lost chances to vex and distress us, we were, I should think, the two saddest prisoners in Germany.

It was a great shock to me to see the change in Baschwitz when on the fifth day we met outside our cells, preparatory to our journey back to Magdeburg. He was, as I have said, a very heavy smoker, and five days without even a cigarette had made him quite ill. He was very pale and his eyes were bloodshot, but he cheered up a little when we met. The escort detailed to conduct us back consisted of a Feldwebel and two privates. The latter were not bad fellows, but the Feldwebel was the most complete brute it has ever been my misfortune to meet. He insisted on searching us, though he was told it was quite unnecessary, and he did it in the most insulting way possible, and then, having got us outside, told us, shouting at the top of his voice, that he forbade us to speak to each other, and that if he had the slightest reason to suspect us of attempting to get away, he would have us shot there in the street. As we marched along he constantly bawled out to the crowd that we were prisoners of war who had broken our parole, and that we were being taken to Magdeburg to be executed. On reaching the station we found the train not yet in, so we were pushed into a corner and people were invited to come and look at us. Never during my captivity have I felt so acutely the shame of my position as I did then, and Baschwitz and I could not look each other in the face during that journey. I suppose that the man who deliberately made this our worst day in Germany has long since fallen on the field. If so, it was a better death than he deserved!

It took us about twelve hours to reach our destination, and we were then marched straight to the military prison. During that whole day we had had nothing whatever to eat, but, having been searched for the umpteenth time, we were at last given some bread and locked in our cells. I found myself in the same one as I had occupied during my three days' imprisonment, and it was practically the smallest of all. I think I should have slept little that night, but as I lay down I had visions of our being sent back to the camp and freeing ourselves again within a few days. The following morning the under-officer in charge brought into my cell some cigarettes which had been sent to Baschwitz and myself by another Englishman, Chichester-Constable, who was undergoing a long sentence – also for an attempt at escape. I shall never forget the delight of that first cigarette, nor how completely my outlook on things changed with the feeling of smoke once more in my lungs.

I do not wish to go into a lengthy description of prison life, nor can I think of any single incident in those three months worth recording. The first ten days were the worst, for during that time we had only such food as the Germans gave us – a loaf to last six days, in the morning coffee, but nothing to eat; at midday a bowl of soup; and for supper a little jam, or a piece of sausage or some smoked fish. We were very lousy, which did not tend to make things any more comfortable, and we constantly asked that our things might be sent down to us. At last they came, and it was with the greatest relief that one got into a clean shirt and into uniform again. Our parcels started to arrive before long, and a certain amount of reading matter was also sent down to us by our friends, but we were never allowed to see or speak to each other, which was very irksome. Our exercise occupied one hour daily, and we were accompanied by a sentry, but the time allotted to me was from seven to eight in the morning, so that it did not serve much to split up the day. Fridays and Saturdays were spent in pleasant anticipations of Sunday's lunch, which was generally a good one. Monday was a bad day, but on Tuesday and Wednesday one was kept busy looking forward to the weekly bath on Thursday! A man can, I suppose, become accustomed to anything, and yet it was with disgust that I realized I was becoming almost resigned to this life. I grew to be able to plan, sitting there in my cell, that I was a free man again and once more at the Front, until it became a reality to me – so much a reality, and so exactly did things afterwards turn out as in my most optimistic dreams I had foreseen, that I often wonder nowadays whether it can really be true, and find myself listening with closed eyes for the sound of a German voice and the beat of a sentry's feet.

It was more than two months before we were told the date of our court-martial, but after that we had not long to wait. We were supplied with copies of the charges against us, and were told that we could employ a lawyer if we wished. We found ourselves accused of conspiracy, and of deliberately damaging Government property – the former being, of course, by far the more serious of the two. Things, however, went well for us at the trial, and we were acquitted of conspiracy, as it was held that neither of us had played an essential rôle with relation to the other. On the second count we were sentenced to eleven weeks' imprisonment, from which was to be deducted the time which we had already spent in prison. This meant that after three weeks we should be transferred to another camp and we were well satisfied, and did not of course appeal.

From this time we were allowed to take our exercise together, and also met other prisoners who, having been in the camp at time of our escape, were able to tell us exactly what had happened. After we had been gone two days, they said, the Belgians had decided that there was no longer any necessity to hide our absence from the Germans, and they had, therefore, replaced the bed in my room and removed Baschwitz's dummy. One can well imagine the delighted expectation with which they awaited roll call. The German officer, seeing my empty bed, inquired who slept there, and was told it was Hardy. Where was Hardy? They did not know. When had he last been seen? Some time ago. Some time? Did they mean twenty minutes or half an hour ago? Oh, no, some days ago! Some *days? Donnerwetter!* He rushed out of the room and ran into the other officer, who was shouting wildy, "Baschwitz is gone!" The Commandant arrived within a few minutes in a towering fury. "It is impossible!" he shouted. "From my camp can they not out-flown be. Fetch the dogs. I say to you that they upon the roof found become will!"

A ladder was accordingly fetched, but no clue was discovered. The following day detectives were sent for but, finding nothing, they ordered all grass around the camp to be cut down. It was while engaged on this task that the men discovered the sawn-through planks. No other prisoner had taken advantage of this outlet, but probably no one was ready.

I remember that as the time of our release drew near the days and nights seemed to become of interminable length. It was now September, and we had spent the best of the summer behind bars, and were desperately-anxious to get to work again. Our only fear was that we might be separated and sent to different camps, for it was not usual to leave escape partners together. Our sentence expired at eight o'clock in the evening, but we were not to leave the prison till the following morning. Punctually, however, at 8 p.m. when we ceased to be officially under arrest, our cell doors were opened, and we were told that we could have free access to the corridor. We also received the joyful tidings that we were to be sent together to Burg, near Madgeburg. We spent the whole night walking arm in arm up and down the corridor, completely delighted at the turn of events and full of ideas for the future. It did not seem possible that with the experience we possessed and with the intense confidence we had in each other, that we could ever fail again. No matter how hard the camp, or how great the distance to be covered, we would do it – most certainly we would do it!

Alas! it was not to be. Scarcely had we arrived at Burg and made our first survey of the camp, when I was sent for to be told that a wire had come through from the Kriegsministerium, ordering that I should be sent to Fort Zorndorf, Küstrin. This came as the greatest shock to both of us, and for a time I really felt that I had no more heart for the game. So much of friendship and understanding had grown up between us that it seemed as though we should be lost and helpless, without each other. And what consolation, we wondered, would it bring to either of us, should he get away, knowing that he left the other still in distress? We spent the whole evening together, but our talk and laughter were forced, and the knowledge that we must say goodbye soon hung over us like a cloud. I was to leave very early in the morning and Baschwitz would not be able to see me then, for prisoners were obliged to keep to their rooms till seven o'clock. I walked over with him to the building in which he slept, and as we reached it the bugle sounded for roll call. We shook hands, and I left him standing there under the arc lamps – the best man I ever knew.

Chapter Twelve

I had often heard of Fort Zorndorf, and I tried to picture to myself what the place would be like as the train whirled us towards Berlin. It was one of the outlying forts of Küstrin – that I knew – and 1 had also heard that no prisoner had ever succeeded in escaping from there. It was reserved for officers – English, Russian and French – whose characters were such that it was not considered wise to leave them in an ordinary camp, and I had no doubt that, once there, I should remain there till the end of the War, unless I could myself work out my own salvation.

We had to cross Berlin on foot to reach the Schlesischer Bahnhof, and did not arrive in Küstrin till late afternoon. We had a four mile uphill tramp from the town to the camp, which lay among the woods, but at last we reached some wooden barracks in which I was told a certain number of the Landsturm men lived, and here we were directed to the outer gate of the fort. The sentry admitted us and we passed down an incline, between massive iron railings, to a second gate, but as it was some time before we were allowed to pass through I had an opportunity of glancing round. We were at the bottom of a huge dry moat, which I afterwards found surrounded the whole fort, and the only means of exit or of entrance to the place was by the gates through which we had passed. The depth of this great ditch was, I should imagine, about forty feet, and its walls were of brick. From here we were led through various underground passages, lighted only at intervals by dim oil lamps, and eventually reached the orderly room. It appeared to me that only a small part of the fort was occupied by prisoners, for up to now we had seen only Germans, of whom there appeared to be a great number – there were, in fact, two hundred men with four officers, though there were rarely more than half that number of prisoners in the camp.

The staff here seemed to be quite well disposed towards one, and I was searched in a very inoffensive manner and was given, during this operation, such information as I wished for; there were eight Englishmen besides myself at Zorndorf, about forty French, a few Belgians and sixty Russians. Roll call, they told me, was held twice daily in the rooms; a cold shower could be had at most times of the day if one cared to pump one's own water, and a hot bath, as far as I remember, once a week. In this camp, unlike all others, German money was allowed, for escape was considered impossible, and the Germans were also convinced that, had they issued tokens, they would have been reproduced by the prisoners within a very short time.

An under-officer came with me to show me my room, and we followed a long underground corridor which led from the orderly room into a courtyard packed with prisoners in every state of déshabillé, for it was a warm evening. One must think of the fort as a great mound of earth – flat topped and surrounded by a deep ditch. Down through the middle of this mound is dug a long narrow pit, the bottom of which is on the same level as the bottom of the ditch. Two sides of this pit are sheer brick walls, the third is formed by the face of the building in which the prisoners lived – two stories and then twenty to twenty-five feet of solid earth; and the fourth side consists of a very steep grass-covered slope, which rises to the height of the fort. At the foot of this slope is a thick barbed wire entanglement with a gate in it, which is closed at nights. This pit which I have described forms the courtyard in which I now found myself.

Of the English in the camp there were two whom I had previously known, and I met one or two old friends among the other nationalities. They were, I suppose, the best crowd of prisoners one could possibly meet – the majority of them young, and most of them men who had already made more than one attempt to get away. Garros – the well known French aviator – was the oldest inhabitant of the place, for most people were not kept there for more than eight months, it having been found that the camp was very depressing and harmful to the prisoners' health. It was not in the true sense of the word a *Strafelager*, but it was what the Germans called a "camp of cure". Their idea was that a man who had spent a certain time there would not make any further efforts to escape on being sent to another camp, for fear of finding himself once more in Zorndorf. In this supposition they were entirely wrong, for the fort came to be called "The Escape University", and there was more to be learned there on that subject than in all the other "Lagers" in Germany put together. One met here men who had actually seen the frontier, and could give most valuable information as to the disposition of sentries at certain points. Others one met who could make a pair of wire-cutters out of a safety razor, a metal saw out of an officer's epaulette, or a complete German uniform out of a Russian greatcoat and a Frenchman's breeches. I felt myself very young and innocent and was ready to learn everything they would teach me, although I suppose there were few among them who had been as fortunate as I had over my break outs; and none, perhaps, to whom I would have given best in the matter of picking a lock! What queer accomplishments! and yet the man who could fashion a key from a piece of his bedstead was greater among us than the famous lawyer who slept beside him and was such a "dud "with his hands!

For three months prior to my arrival work had been carried on unceasingly on a tunnel which was to run from one of the bedrooms on the ground floor, to pass under the moat, and then, mounting upwards, to finish among the trees which surrounded the fort. It was a colossal undertaking, for the greatest difficulty was experienced in supplying air to those working undergound and in disposing of the earth excavated. For this last reason they had been chary of enlarging it at any single point, and for the most part it was just sufficiently large to allow of a man crawling along on his stomach. Work was continued day and night with only a break for roll calls, and after digging about a hundred yards they had encountered water, and had baled for weeks with no effect. Conceive yourself spending from three to six hours daily, flat on your tummy, in a pitch-black hole, crawling backwards and forwards with a tin full of water, which constantly upsets as you push it before you in the sand. Conceive yourself working there day after day, working for an hour after the foul air has extinguished the candle twenty yards behind you, working with the prospect of hearing every moment that the Germans are in the room and you are all discovered. Conceive yourself going down when your turn came, as many did, knowing that you had caught consumption, because you coughed incessantly and spat blood. Imagine the man at the face who dug and dug and tried to forget that at any moment the roof behind him might collapse, and that nothing then could save him from a horrible death in the bowels of the fort. Realize that they loved it, and that they thought it well worth while because it *might* be the means of getting one or two men back to the War!

The whole affair had been discovered by the Germans just a week before I arrived, but luck was with the prisoners to a certain extent, for the room had been raided at a moment when the tunnel had been evacuated for lack of air. The satisfaction on the part of the prisoners that no one had been caught was so great as almost to counteract their sorrow at the loss of all their work, but I found the majority of them very tired out and disappointed, and was told by most of them that there was nothing to be done but to wait until one was transferred to another camp.

I was told all this within the first few hours, and such other efforts as had been made there were also described to me. An attempt had been carried out by a Russian officer, who had disguised himself as a German captain, hoping thus to deceive the sentries at the gates, but this, like everything else, had failed. No matter what method was employed, one was always faced with the difficulty of crossing the ditch, unless some means be found of inducing three separate sentries, on three separate gates, to allow one through. All this sounded rather discouraging, but I could not reconcile myself to the idea that I should be obliged, like the others, to give it up, so went to bed that night with a not altogether unpleasant anticipation of what the morrow might show me.

I was up early the following morning and, finding the gate in the entanglement already unlocked, was able to mount on to the fort by means of a ramp which ran at an angle up the slope.

The fort looked very picturesque in the early morning sunlight, and was quite unlike any other place in which I had ever been confined in its lack of barbed wire and palings; things which one generally associated with a prisoners' camp. There was little stonework to be seen, for all the gun sheds had a protective covering of earth over them, and one received the impression of an irregular mass of grass-covered mounds and trenches among which ran gravel paths. In the centre of it all one looked down into the courtyard, and the whole was enclosed by the great moat. The first question which one asked oneself – probably the first question that every prisoner asked himself on arriving at Zorndorf – was what possibility would there be of using a ladder, supposing that one were able to construct one of sufficient length. Numerous sentries were dotted about, and on walking from post to post one began to realize that they had been very carefully placed, and that they held between them every inch of the ditch under view. It might, however, be possible to divert their attention during a stunt, I thought, and I went down to roll call with more than one idea maturing in my mind.

That afternoon I was destined to gain a conception of how very effective were the defences of the camp. I was told, only of course in the strictest confidence, and merely because I was the only man in the fort who didn't know, that two Russians were about to make an attempt to break out by means of a rope which they had made, and to the end of which had been attached a grapnel. Although the outer side of the moat was a sheer brick wall, the inner side, at certain points, was simply a precipitous grass slope down which, if unobserved, one could slide and so reach the bottom of the ditch. Should they succeed in getting so far, they then intended to fling up their grapnel in such a way as to engage with some iron railings outside the moat. Whether it would be possible to draw the attention of the sentries long enough to enable them to do this, to climb the rope, and then, having drawn it up behind them, to disappear into the woods, appeared very doubtful, but two of the English in my room had offered their services for this purpose. It had been arranged that they should start a fight in the vicinity of one of the sentry's posts, while some Frenchmen, armed with two cats in a small closed basket, were to create a diversion at another point and, watches having been carefully compared, we mounted to the top of the fort. I have omitted to say that a sentry was posted on the ramp up which one was obliged to go, and played here a more important role than one at first imagined, for it was necessary to pass within a yard or two of him, and he could not fail to see if one carried anything suspicious about one. This of course explained why no attempt had ever been made with a ladder.

I did not feel justified in watching the show too closely for fear of drawing attention to what was happening; and so, excited though I was, I kept well away from the Russians' starting point and walked slowly towards a group of prisoners, in the centre of which two Englishmen were engaged in titanic combat. The sentry who stood near appeared very interested, though he occasionally glanced round his sector, but as the fight waxed in fury he seemed to become entirely engrossed in it.

One felt that one simply must go and see what was happening, and it was only with the greatest effort that one could resist the temptation. The heart of every prisoner went out to those two down in the ditch, and at the sudden sound of a shout in the distance the faces of those standing near me became a real study in anxiety and pity. The sentry laughed as he looked down at us and cried:

"Jetzt können sie aufhören, meine Herren; die haben ihn schon fest!" ("You can stop now, gentlemen, they've caught him!").

Imagine one's mortification at finding that all one's efforts had never succeeded in deceiving him for a moment! I translated what he had said, and think he must have got a lot of satisfaction from the red and angry faces he saw below him, but he had spoken the truth, and as we walked along the top we saw the two unfortunates led off under guard. They had, we were told, successfully descended the slope, but had scarcely crossed the bottom of the ditch and prepared to throw their rope before they were seen and challenged by a sentry, who should really have had his whole attention occupied in watching the cat fight organized by the French!

All this served to show me that people were perfectly correct in saying that it was foolishness to attempt anything here during the day, but I began to ask myself whether a repetition of the Russians' attempt, carried out by night, would have better hopes of success. I made most careful inquiries as to the method adopted by the

Germans for guarding the place after dark, and found them very severe indeed. A few minutes before evening roll call, which varied with the time of year, but was invariably held before dusk, an under-officer with some men was detailed to clear the top of the fort of prisoners, who were obliged then to descend into the courtyard. The Germans having satisfied themselves that everybody was there and that no one had hidden himself in the grass, the sentries closed in round the mouth of the pit, while at the same time others marched on to their beats in the moat, which was lighted at intervals by oil lamps. These men were withdrawn at daylight, and the others then fell back on to their day posts; and having mastered these facts I was not altogether surprised at Zorndorf's remarkable record, and began to wonder if I was not now confronted with too tough a proposition.

The following day I was introduced to an old French captain of great renown, whom I shall call Midi; this man had made, according to his own account, something like twenty attempts to escape, but had always been betrayed, with the result that he had never once succeeded in getting clear of a camp. He was remarkable in that he never *failed,* but was always *betrayed,* and I have constantly heard him say that the Germans employed spies especially to watch him. He was a man of many years' service, with much experience of colonial warfare, and was, I am sure, a very valiant soldier. He was bald and wore a heavy moustache and most disreputable clothes; was a hard worker and clever with his hands, grumbled incessantly, and was the most complete liar I have ever had the privilege of meeting. He was by no means popular among the other prisoners, for he was most insulting on occasions, and would accuse his brother officers of being spies on the slightest provocation. Midi had been a long time in the camp, and I spent many hours in his company discussing various schemes and finding nothing which could possibly be considered feasible. In one thing, and in one thing only, was the Zorndorf prisoner more fortunate than his brothers. There was a Russian tailor in the camp who had much work to do for the Germans, and in this way he was able to acquire a certain amount of cast-off German uniform. He was also allowed to buy a limited quantity of cloth from the town, and the obtaining of civilian clothes became for us therefore a very simple affair. The Germans were well aware of what went on, but as no one ever succeeded in breaking out, and as everybody was searched before leaving the camp with the result that these things fell into the Germans hands, it was almost to their advantage to allow this state of affairs to continue.

I scarcely know to whom to attribute the scheme on which we at last found ourselves working, but I believe that it was originally invented in a rather vague form by another Frenchman. This man had most unwisely revealed his idea to my friend, and he for some time had pondered over it, saying nothing to me, and then one day had taken the other aside and had spoken. To begin with – it was so exactly like him – he had pooh-poohed the whole plan, and had then begun gradually to point out how totally unsuited his listener was for such an affair, and how essential it had become that every opportunity should be given himself of returning to the Front. He was a captain – an officer very ancient – the other was merely a subaltern … I saw the poor little Frenchman shortly after this conversation had taken place. He looked somewhat dazed and a little sad, for he had liked his scheme, though I doubt myself whether he would ever have put it to the test. Be that as it may, the point was that he had renounced all claim to it and so passes out of this story.

The fort was, as I have said, divided into two parts – that in which we lived and that occupied by the Germans – and there were only two legitimate ways by which one could pass from one to the other. At one end of the courtyard an underground passage ran down to the orderly room, while in the middle of the yard was the opening of a corridor which ran the whole length of the fort, and was, so to speak, its main artery. At the point where this corridor debouched into the yard was a high gate with a wicket, and the sentry mounted here had orders to allow no one through whom he did not actually recognize as being one of the staff. This way therefore was out of the question. The orderly room, on the other hand, had two doors, one opening into our part of the fort, and the other opening into a passage to which prisoners had not access. Now half way down to the orderly room there was a door in the wall which had been nailed up and behind which had been built a strong wooden barricade which reached up to the ceiling. By incessantly questioning orderlies we had discovered that, could we make our way through these two obstructions, we should find ourselves in the passage which contained the second door of the orderly room and those of the kitchen and German wash room. Following it along one would strike the main corridor and then, turning to the right, would reach the two outer gates of the fort. We intended to make our attempt disguised as German soldiers, and we hoped and trusted that these disguises would be sufficiently good to deceive the sentries at the gates, for their orders were not so strict as those issued to the man at the wicket in the courtyard. The first thing to be done was to arrange about our kits, and it was with relief that we learned that only fatigue dress would be necessary. The Landsturm men, when off duty, generally wore white canvas jackets, corduroy trousers with red piping and the small round field service cap. These the tailor made for us within a few days; and we then set him at work on our civilian clothes.

It was now November and beginning to get very cold. Four of the English had already been transferred to another camp, and one new one, by name Breen, had arrived. I had known the latter well in the early days of captivity, and knew also that he spoke fluent German and had made several attempts to escape. I therefore suggested to Midi that Breen would be a very useful man in such an affair. Midi agreed with me and I found Breen only too delighted at the prospect, and explained the plan to him. For some time we had been studying the movements of the Germans immediately after evening roll call, and had found that it was at this time that all those not on duty went to the kitchen to fetch their evening meal. They waited in a queue in the passage to which we hoped to gain access, but there was a slight turn in the latter which would, we hoped, suffice to screen us from their view as we crawled through the barricade. Those of the Germans who lived in the barracks outside the camp then carried their food away and were allowed through the gates. Our plan was to break into the passage and join these men as they left the kitchen, follow them down the main corridor, and then march out of the camp among them, for it seemed improbable that three new faces would be noticed by the sentry among so many. We were all agreed that, once safely through the barricade, this looked the easiest stunt we had ever tried.

It was now time we got to work, and choosing our moment one evening, we succeeded with great difficulty in withdrawing two of the huge nails which had been used to fix the door. We cut these down and replaced the heads, for it was essential that the door should bear no traces of having been tampered with. The following evening we got out the remainder of the nails, and after some minutes of fumbling, succeeded in picking the lock and opening the door; but after a hasty glance inside closed it again and fixed it with two screws, for we did not intend to commence work on the barricade until everything else was ready. In the short space of time during which the door was open I had been able to satisfy myself that there would be sufficient room between the two obstacles to allow of myself – the smallest member of the party – being shut in there to work during the day. We had decided that work at night would be impossible on account of the noise, and it was clear that, even by day, I must take the greatest precautions.

In the meanwhile Breen was at work on an attempt to produce passes which would enable us to travel safely by train, for we understood that the railways were becoming every day more strictly supervised. With the help of a Russian he had made out a certain formula, though it remained to be seen whether it was anything approaching the correct one. There was a typewriter in the camp, and another Russian who was very skilful with his fingers had cut some stamps in rubber, and these gave impressions somewhat similar to those seen on passports issued by the police. Ink was made out of indelible pencil, and, though the stamps were of course rather crude, the papers when finished had quite a business-like appearance.

We were in poor spirits about this time, though we felt more sure of success than we ever had before. The Somme battle had been raging for some months, but had now died down, and we feared that Britain's great stroke had failed. The German papers were full of the "unrestricted U Boat Warfare", and one really began to ask oneself whether we could ever win. Those were days indeed when one needed something to occupy one's mind; days when every letter from home spoke of some new loss, and we were very hard on ourselves, believe me, that we were not there to take our share. One day, while I was walking alone in the yard, some one threw down a letter which had just arrived for me. It was from my people and it bore the news of Baschwitz's escape, for he had spent a day with them while in England. This was my first intimation; indeed, I had been daily expecting his arrival in the fort, and though I was – for him – utterly delighted, the contrast between his position and mine smote me with such a sense of depression and despair as I have seldom experienced. He was the better man, more capable, steadier;

he deserved it far more than I, yet the thought of it preyed on my mind, and the knowledge that I had done my last stunt with him came as a hard blow. I did not hear from him; indeed, I never heard from him until I too was a free man, but he did not need to explain to me when we met. It was a piece of understanding of which no man would have been capable who did not feel towards captivity as we two felt.

Chapter Thirteen

We did not waste a moment after the tailor had completed our outfits, but went down together one morning and, at a moment when the passage was empty, unscrewed the door; and then, having made sure that I had the necessary tools with me, I got in, and the others drove the screws into place again. I had only such light there as came between the planks, but this was no new form of work to me, and I started to cut a hole for the saw precisely as we had done at Magdeburg. I was able to watch what went on in the passage, and this I did persistently, stopping work each time I saw anyone approaching. There was a constant stream of Germans to and from the orderly room and I made in consequence very slow progress, with the result that when I was let out, stiff and hungry, in time for evening roll call, I had only done about one-third of the task.

It was in fact four days before the job was completed, and I had the satisfaction of re-moving the piece of plank and pushing my head through into the forbidden passage. I swept up all the sawdust which lay, and which might possibly draw attention to what had been done, and then replaced the board, screwing another across it to retain it in position. There was great satisfaction and excitement when my two fellow conspirators let me out that evening and heard that I had finished, and we held a dress rehearsal that night, examining each other critically both in German kit and in civilians, and coming to the conclusion that all were excellent. Midi looked his part of a Landsturm man to a nicety, and though he spoke no single word of German, his appearance should be almost enough to pull him through. Compass, maps, food; everything in order; and now to possess our souls in patience until the following evening.

I do not pretend that I felt anything but the old nervousness as I lay on my bed twenty four hours later waiting for evening roll call. Often at these moments I have compared my feelings with those of a man waiting in the front line trenches for the signal to attack, and have thought how little worse is his position than that of a prisoner about to take the plunge. One cannot, of course, compare the risks run in the two cases, but my own experience shows me that the mental strain is far greater in the case of the prisoner, and two or three attempts in a year were just about as much as the average man could stand.

The moment roll call was finished we hurried out into the courtyard and met Bastin, a Belgian who had promised to help us. We wore our military greatcoats over our German uniforms and under the latter we wore complete civilians, and it can well be imagined how bulky and helpless we felt as we walked slowly down the passage, while Bastin, who had run on ahead, was unfixing the door. Needless to say, it was essential that we should not be seen loitering about here, and therefore the moment the door was opened we pulled off our greatcoats and crowded into the narrow space between the door and the barricade. Bastin handed us the plates and bowls which we intended to carry in order to complete the illusion, and then, with the greatest difficulty, he closed the door and started to drive the screws again. With three of us packed in that tiny space we had not room to raise a finger, and it was only by employing all my strength in forcing the other two against the wall that I made sufficient place to kneel down and get to my work. I had a small screwdriver with me, and had just finished unfixing the plank when I heard Bastin pick up the coats and walk away, having completed his task.

We were all dripping with perspiration by now, and in spite of the most desperate endeavours it began to appear as though I could not back away sufficiently from the hole to get my head and shoulders through. I heard Breen suggest to Midi that the latter should get out and postpone his twenty first attempt, though how it was proposed that he should make his exit I do not know. Midi's reply was furious in the extreme, and he never forgot or forgave this effort to deprive him of the fruits of what he always called *his* plan! At last, and only after as big a fight as I ever remember making, I managed to squeeze myself through and get to my feet on the other side. The head of the queue of Germans was within a few yards of us, but just round the bend of the passage, and I prayed inwardly that none of them would stroll round before my two companions were through and the plank in place again. Midi had a harder task than either Breen or myself, for he was inclined to be stout and would, I think, never have succeeded but for our help. However, after a terrific struggle, we got him through, and having closed the hole picked up our crockery and walked boldly in among the Germans.

Not a word was said as we pushed past the queue towards the wash room, and nobody appeared in the slightest suspicious of us. The soup was already being served out and we had not long to wait before a number of men passed us, coming from the kitchen, and turned into the main corridor. We followed them, carrying our bowls with a plate over them, as we saw the Germans doing, in order to keep their meal warm, and though we passed several sentries no one so much as glanced at us, and we became every moment more confident.

And now we made our first bad blunder. The group of Germans which we had been following was by now some distance ahead of us, but we decided not to run in order to catch up, fearing to draw attention to ourselves, and the result was that on reaching the first gate we found to our consternation that the last man had passed through and that it was closed. Nothing that we could say appeared to have the slightest effect on the sentry, who, not recognizing us as belonging to the garrison, refused to open the gate for us until he received instructions from the guardroom. This was a terrible shock to us and, completely taken aback, we turned and started to retrace our steps. We walked slowly, for we were absolutely unable to decide what our next move should be, and our one idea had become to get back into our part of the camp and avoid capture. A German officer – one of the camp staff – passed us on his way down to the gate, and we saluted him, and then, I know not why, turned and followed him. He, too, had passed through before we reached it again, but Breen, in a fit of extraordinary boldness, shouted after him; "Herr Leutnant! Herr Leutnant!" He did not hear, but the sentry of course heard and, with his suspicions completely lulled by this piece of bluff, threw the gate open, to our complete astonishment, and allowed us through! I cannot describe the extraordinary revulsion of feeling which one experienced at that moment. Thirty seconds before we had been in the depths of despair – had given up all hope and had resigned ourselves to the humiliation of failure – and then the unforeseen – a slight chance offered and seized … I felt I could have hugged Breen for what he had done as we walked towards the outer gate, our last obstacle.

We were now in the open air, and this fact made us realize the more how near we were to freedom. It was quite dark but for the dim rays of an oil lamp which hung from the railings, and by its light we could see a group of fifteen or twenty German soldiers standing there waiting to pass out to their barracks. It was raining slightly, but the sentry stood obstinately barring the way; and, in answer to their complaints that their food was growing cold, he replied that he was forbidden to allow anyone through until the corporal of the guard arrived. Breen and I began to grumble to each other in German, and an N.C.O. who stood near remarked to us that the rules of the fort were very strict, and that he himself could not quit the place without permission. We told him that we had only joined the company that evening, and on being asked to which room we had been posted we answered that we were to sleep in No. 1, for we had no idea how many rooms there were in the barracks. After this he seemed, to our relief, to lose interest in us, and no one spoke to us again until the corporal arrived from the guardroom, and he merely glanced over the group and then signalled to the sentry to open the gate. Intensely excited, yet necessarily appearing indifferent, we moved forward casually with the rest, and I remember that I yawned, for the eyes of the corporal were upon us. For one glorious moment I thought he half turned as though to go, and then, suddenly stepping in front of us, he said:

"You three have only arrived this evening, ja?"

"Ja, Herr Unter Ofhzier, sind heute abend angekommen," I answered.

"Have you got your supper all right?" he asked.

"Jawohl."

"What have they given you today?"

"Potato soup and sausage," I said, and then added, "At least that's what we were told we should get, but the others have drawn ours for us."

I was obliged to say this, for our bowls were empty, and had he asked to see what we had in them his suspicions would have been aroused on finding we had lied to him.

"Donnerwetter!" he answered. "You fellows cannot have been soldiering long if you allow yourselves to be swindled like that. You'll have to come back with me, and I will report to the Feldwebel and try and get you some soup."

This is the worst which could possibly have happened, for, although our disguises were good, they had never been intended to bear scrutiny, and we were convinced that the moment we were seen in the light we should be detected. Breen took up the tale, and argued that the man who had promised to fetch our food was a personal friend of his, and would not dream of swindling us. But it was all of no avail; we were in Germany, and it was an order that every man must draw his own rations, and having failed to do this yet we must return and draw them now.

We could not refuse, for had we done so we should have been arrested immediately, so we were forced to follow him back into the fort, though only with the darkest forebodings. None of this conversation had been understood by poor Midi, and he always maintained afterwards that he had suffered far more acutely during the whole affair than either Breen or myself. On reaching the main corridor the corporal led us up a passage to the right and, opening a door, pushed us into a small and overheated room, in which sat a Feldwebel writing at a table.

"Herr Feldwebel," said the corporal, "here are three new Landsturm men who have been swindled out of their rations."

The man looked up, surprised to see three men of the garrison whose faces he did not know, and remarking that he had never seen us before he pulled a slip of papers towards him and asked me my name:

"Bruno Schulte," I answered.

"Herman Eibenstein," said Breen, indicating himself in the approved German manner.

"And yours?" said the Feldwebel, turning to Midi.

Now Midi, as I have said, spoke no single word of German, but he had understood the question. For a moment I saw a look of pain cross his face, and then he uttered a loud and guttural growl.

"What?" asked the Feldwebel. "How do you spell it?"

But this was Breen's cue, and in a moment he had spelt out a name which apparently satisfied the Feldwebel, for he wrote it down on his paper and then, getting up, moved towards the door. To get there he had to pass us, and as he did so he stopped with a jerk. We stood rigidly to attention as he looked us up and down, examining our cap badges and staring at our boots. He said afterwards that his first idea on realizing that we were not what we pretended to be was that we were spies who had, in some way, effected an entrance to the camp. Be that as it may, he suddenly went white in the face and cried:

"Arrest them!"

"Why?" said the corporal.

"Arrest them, I tell you!" he repeated, backing into a corner and looking perfectly terrified.

The corporal appeared completely puzzled, but he turned us about and marched us up another passage. He confided to me on the way that the Feldwebel was a fool, and that he himself did not wish to arrest us at all. However, orders were orders ... We reached the end of the passage and here he opened a door, and we found ourselves in a room full of Landsturm men, all of whom glanced up at us as we entered.

"Three new chaps," said the corporal again, "who have been swindled out of their food." Some of the men laughed, but the majority did not seem interested in us, and we stood awkwardly by the door, wondering what steps the Feldwebel was taking. It was plain to us now that all was lost, and thinking it better to discover ourselves to them rather than allow them to find out I turned to the N.C.O., after a whispered word to my companions, and said:

"It's no good keeping up the pretence. We're prisoners of war, you know!"

I would rather draw a curtain over the scene which followed.

Suffice it to say that we had an exceedingly noisy and unpleasant half-hour, lost all our civilian clothes, our maps and the compass, and found ourselves in a remarkably short space of time marching down to Küstrin gaol under a strong escort.

Our disgust and disappointment were beyond all words. This was the first time I had ever failed to make a clean get away, and I began to fear that my luck was getting still worse. It was terribly cold; snow lay thick upon the ground, and it was very slippery underfoot. Oh, Lord! how miserable I felt!

"Betrayed!" said Midi.

Chapter Fourteen

Much to our astonishment we were informed, after being in prison for a few days, that the authorities did not intend to take action against us, and that in a short time we should return to the fort. It was, however, pointed out that what we had done would very much prejudice our chances of being transferred to another camp, and this was indeed a bad hearing. I became at once eager to get back, not only on account of the fact that we were short of food and not allowed to smoke, but because I felt that I had by no means exhausted my resources, and that I should before long be able to devise some new scheme. I think our whole imprisonment did not last more than ten days, but we were delighted when the time expired, and our spirits were very much higher as we set out on our four mile march to the fort than they had been on that disastrous evening.

Everything in the camp was much as we had left it, with the exception of the barricade, which had been replaced by a brick wall, covered with a layer of strong cement. One Englishman who had been some eight months at Zorndorf had been transferred elsewhere, and a new flying man had arrived, called Duncan Grinnell-Milne, with a head of flaming red hair and a wonderful German accent. He, like most other "Zorndorfians", had made several attempts to get away.

The weather was now colder than I had ever before known it, and we used to spend the greater part of the day in bed, planning and rehearsing incessantly. It was about this time that I made my first attempt at cutting rubber stamps, though I found myself, to begin with, unable to produce anything as good even as those made by the

Russian (who had left the camp), and *they* were crude enough in all conscience! I used safety razor blades for carving the rubber, and after persevering for some weeks found myself improving, though the results fell far short of what could be desired.

Bastin, who had helped us in our last attempt, mentioned to me one day that he and Garros, the aviator, had devised a plan which had, he thought, every prospect of succeeding. The fact, however, that the ground was still deeply covered with snow necessitated their postponing it, and it seemed likely that Garros would be transferred to another camp before the thaw, in which case Bastin suggested that he and I should make the attempt together. I was very grateful to him for this; and, although I had a very shrewd idea of the outline of his scheme, his kindness of course barred me from doing anything likely to prejudice it.

In the meantime we had been discussing in our room the advisability of attempting a bolt while being conducted to the Kommandatur, which was outside the camp. The whole fort was surrounded by woods, and we felt that given even half a minute's start it would be very difficult for the Germans to lay hands on us again. Bolting is, as a rule, a very unsatisfactory method, as it is difficult to fit oneself out properly beforehand, and the alarm is given immediately; also it invariably results in the guard being punished, which is not in the interest of prisoners. Eventually, however, we three, Breen, Duncan and myself, decided that under the circumstances it was justifiable, and chose the 3rd January as the fatal day.

I do not intend to write fully of this affair, for an account has already appeared in print.[1] Suffice it to say that Duncan and myself got clear away, but Breen was unfortunately captured in the first

1. See "An Escaper's Log," by Duncan Grinnell-Milne. (The Bodley Head.)

rush after being well fired at for his pains, though he was not hit. We spent a terrible night tramping through the woods in the pouring rain, and at last reached a railway station many miles from Küstrin, where, draggled and suspicious as we looked, we succeeded in buying tickets. We soon realized however that the pursuit of us this time had been organized with unprecedented thoroughness, and the *denouement* of our experiences was reached when I suddenly found myself looking down the barrel of a revolver levelled at me by an apparently inoffensive fellow passenger – a burly civilian, who turned out to be a police agent. So we found ourselves once more in Küstrin gaol, and it was the end of January before we returned to the camp, having won for ourselves the undying hatred of the Commandant. I in particular was so exceedingly obnoxious to him that he could never afterwards bring himself to pronounce my name, and always referred to me as "the Irish officer "or "Leutnant Dings" – otherwise Lieutenant Thingummy!

Things began now to look very black for us. We had behaved impudently, but we had done what appeared to us right at the time, and, having forfeited any consideration at the hands of the Germans in the way of transfer to another camp, we felt that our only hope was to continue in our efforts. Bastin had now developed his scheme to me, and it certainly seemed most ingenious and quite worthy of him, for he was one of the most brilliant escapers in Germany.

There was a long passage which led from our part of the fort to a small chapel, the barred window's of which were set, so to speak, in the slope, by means of which the Russians, as will be remembered, had descended into the ditch. The Germans were in the habit of examining the bars daily, and any question of cutting them through could not therefore arise, but there was a door which, though strongly barricaded, offered certain possibilities. Bastin had been at work here for several days, and had succeeded not only in cutting a hole in the door sufficiently large for a man to crawl through, but had also most cleverly concealed every trace of his work. Any attempt to get out of this chapel during the day would inevitably be frustrated, as, shortly after the Russians' escapade, the Germans had posted a sentry immediately above it. During the night, however, one stood a good chance of crawling out unseen, and this done one would have access to the ditch. Now Bastin, like all other Zorndorfians, had definitely decided that the presence of the sentries in the moat precluded any attempt to scale the wall, and he had seen no way of overcoming this difficulty, until he made by accident a remarkable discovery. The sentries in question were recalled from their posts at dawn, and we had always taken it for granted that those surrounding the mouth of the courtyard fell back at the same moment on to their day posts, from which they commanded the moat. This, however, was not the case; for before doing so they were accustomed to wait until word was brought them from the guardroom that the ditch was evacuated, and the result was that for some three minutes every morning it remained completely unguarded.

Bastin's plan was to hide himself in the chapel and allow the Germans to lock him in there for the night; to crawl out while it was still dark, carrying with him a ladder built in sections; to choose some lonely spot on top of the fort where undisturbed he could put his ladder together; and then, the moment the sentries had left the ditch, to descend into it and scale the wall. There were two cupboards in the tiny chapel, and these were invariably kept locked by the French priest and fastened with padlocks. Bastin thought that the fact of these having been obviously locked from the outside would prevent the Germans suspecting that any prisoner would hide in them, as he considered it improbable that the under-officer who made the rounds would know as much as he did about the extreme simplicity of manipulating a lock from the *inside!* and he had so arranged one of the cupboards as to be able to do this. It was, of course, possible that the Germans were even more thorough in their examination of the place than he knew, but there was nothing for it, as the passage which led to the chapel was barred by iron gates, which were locked after evening roll call and periodically examined during the night, and we did not feel ourselves equal to effecting an entrance through these.

The ladder, which had been made by Garros, was constructed out of deck-chair frames and the iron bars used to support the boards of our barrack-room beds. It was built in several sections, and after every piece had been carefully fitted and numbered, the irons had all been replaced in the various beds from which they had been taken, there to remain until the day of the escape.

I remember most clearly that day in February, 1917, when Garros received the news that his transfer had come through. He, poor fellow, was dreadfully cut up that he was not able to profit by all his work, but he considered it out of the question to make the attempt while snow still lay thick upon the ground, so he was obliged to leave in the depths of gloom. It is good to know that he did at last gain his heart's desire, and though he was killed within three months of gaining his freedom he fell in battle on French soil, and finds himself among a very glorious company. *Requiescat in pace.*

I spent the whole of that evening with Bastin, and succeeded in persuading him that there was no reason whatever why three should not work the scheme together, and when once this was agreed upon I fetched Duncan and we ran over the whole affair with him. It was while we were actually so engaged that a German from the orderly room came in on some errand or other and casually mentioned to Bastin that he would be leaving the fort in a few days. My friend looked very much dismayed, and the moment the German had departed he turned to me with a long face and said:

"I'm not going to suffer as Garros did. We must go tomorrow, and as for the snow – well, we shall have to spend the morning making white clothes for ourselves."

To Duncan and myself it was immaterial whether the attempt was made at once or a few days later, but we were both so fond of Bastin that the idea of his being sent away, leaving us to take advantage of all his work, was positively repulsive to us, and we agreed most heartily as to the necessity of acting at once. The following day was accordingly spent in collecting our outfits from their respective hiding places, and in borrowing white shirts and flannel trousers to wear over our own black clothes. We even went the length of raising three pairs of white socks to cover our boots with, for the nights were very bright at this time, and the whole success of the scheme depended upon our not being visible against the snow.

The instant evening roll call was finished we ran upstairs and met Bastin in the passage. We had not a moment to waste, and he had scarcely time to lock Duncan and myself into one cupboard and get into the other himself before we heard the Germans coming. The under-officer did not even trouble to examine the padlocks, but simply walked across the tiny room, raised the altar cloth and glanced beneath, and departed; we heard him locking the iron gates behind him as he went. Duncan and I were now so cramped as to be hardly able to move, and it was with the greatest relief that we heard Bastin emerge from his cupboard and unlock ours. Our chief task was now to put together the ladder – the pieces of which we had hidden the previous day in various parts of the room – into such lengths as the size of the place permitted. It was midnight before we had completed the task, and the ladder was then in three sections, which was the most convenient form for carrying it to the other side of the fort, where we intended to make the attempt.

Bastin was a true professional, and had been thorough in his preparations to the extent of providing a saucepan full of soup and a small spirit stove, for it was desperately cold. Having finished with the ladder we decided to heat up the soup, and he went and stood at the window, from where he could see the sentry as he passed on the ramparts, and give us the word to light up. We heard him whisper that all was clear, but I had no sooner struck the match and bent down, shielding the flame with my hands, when he suddenly gave vent to a sort of shout of suppressed horror. In a flash I had extinguished the light and was beside him at the window.

"O–h!" said Bastin with a groan. "Nous sommes pincés!" ("We are caught!").

And then in a miserable whisper he told me what had happened. There had been no one in sight when he had given the word; not a soul – and then as the light flared up the head and shoulders of a sentry had appeared opposite the window, and about fifteen paces distant. He had apparently 'been sheltering in one of the emplacements and had climbed on to the parapet at the moment of my striking the match. I can see him now as he stood there, a grey figure with muffled head – slung rifle – his coat blowing sideways in the bitter wind. We saw him get down into the emplacement again, and mount the parapet once more as though to see whether his eyes had played him a trick, and then he disappeared as suddenly as he had come. For some time we looked at each other, and then Duncan said:

"It would take him at least a minute to report at the guardroom, even if he ran, and it would be another two minutes before they could get here. If no one comes within four minutes, say, we can take it for granted that he thinks his eyes deceived him."

And then we sat still and waited. I had a luminous watch with me, and could check the minutes as they passed. Two – three – four!

S-s-sh! they're coming! The sound of a key in the lock of the first
gate – the tramp of heavy boots in the stone passage – a loud rattling
at the second gate, and then – retreating footsteps and a clang – the
Rounds!

And there we sat and laughed and joked and punched each other
in the dark. Pincés! not by a hundred miles; we'd go a lot farther
before they pinched us!

It was half past two before we had completed our arrangements,
and Bastin then began removing the loose plank in the door. I had
won the toss and was to go first and crawl straight to the other side
of the fort, carrying one section of the ladder, and not waiting for the
others. We were all dressed entirely in white and, clumsy though we
felt on account of the quantity of clothes we were wearing, we were
glad of them, for the cold was intense. I was by now well accustomed
to crawling through small holes, and was out in a moment, while
the others prepared to hand me my section of ladder through the
window. It seemed very long – much longer than I had anticipated
– and miscalculating the point of balance I let the end fall as they
released it, and it crashed among some broken glass which lay
upon the ground. I picked it up again and at once turned with the
intention of getting clear in case I had been heard, and glimpsed as
I did so the two faces of my companions looking white and horrified
in the moonlight. I followed the direction of their gaze, and there
– standing exactly where the last had stood – was a sentry, staring
straight at me.

I did not dare to move. I did not dare even to look frightened,
but simply stood like a rock and wondered where I should be hit –
whether it would hurt much – whether this was the finish. I suppose
I stood there for two minutes, but it seemed like an hour. The sentry
never took his eyes from me, though I realize now that he could

see nothing and had merely heard the noise. And then I glanced up again and he was gone!

Duncan pressed his face against the bars.

"Either that man's a Socialist," he whispered, "or we've seen a miracle! Push on!"

"Push on?" I answered. "Do you think I'm going to stop here after *that?*"and we both laughed.

My little tour round the fort went smoothly, and I finished up in a deep hollow on the far side, where the others joined me a few minutes later. We could still scarcely believe that the sentry had not seen me, but we had no time for surmises, and got to work at once on fixing together the three sections of the ladder. It was so cold that our hands stuck to the ironwork, but somehow we got it done and then sat in a bunch to wait for eight o'clock, the hour at which the ditch was evacuated. We did not suffer nearly so much during this five hours' wait as one would imagine. We could hear the sentries talking to each other in the moat, and occasionally we heard the patrols in the woods outside the fort, but we smoked, lighting one cigarette from the butt end of another, and amusing ourselves with stories of previous attempts.

At dawn we began removing our white clothes, for we should need them no longer, and from then on we spoke no more, but listened most intensely for any sound in the ditch. We looked constantly at our watches, and as the time drew near we placed the ladder ready to our hands. Punctually at eight o'clock we heard a group of sentries talking as they made their way to the guardroom, and that was our signal. Seizing our ladder we literally charged out of the hollow – I could hardly repress a shout as we did so – crossed a flat tongue of land at full speed in a flurry of snow, and, throwing ourselves on our backs, toboganned down into the ditch, having first sent the ladder sliding on its way. We were up in a moment, dashed towards the wall and with the greatest difficulty reared the ladder against it, Duncan and I exerting all our strength to relieve the strain as much as possible, while Bastin started to mount.

The ladder was strong enough and would in normal times have been long enough, for Bastin was able to get his fingers on to the stone ledge, which was all we had expected and considered necessary. But there was a coating of ice over it, and he could get no grip whatever. He just looked down at us with a faint smile and shook his head – and at the same moment a stream of Germans walked out of the guardroom and fell in within fifty yards of us! Bastin descended and, leaving the ladder where it stood, started towards the gate as one last desperate resort, but an N.C.O. stopped us and asked us whether we had come to repair the wall, and if so why we had not reported ourselves.

"Ach! "said Duncan, "that's what we're just going to do."

"Well," said the German, "I'll come with you," and he continued to walk beside us.

As we passed the parade, I saw looks of surprise on many of the soldiers' faces, and one of them called out:

"Why, it's Hardy and Milne," for the latter's flaming red hair was unmistakable.

The under-officer stopped and stared at us. He took off Duncan's hat and, suddenly recognizing him, shouted:

"Donnerwetter! Wieder ein Fluchtver-such hat stattgefunden. Ich hab's nicht gewusst! ich hab's nicht gewusst!" ("Great Scot! Another attempt to escape has taken place. I didn't know! I didn't know!").

"Jawohl," I assented drearily, and amidst a scene of the greatest excitement we entered the guardroom.

One failure is as horrible as another, and there is little to be gained by dwelling on it. We were stripped and made to walk to the other side of the room, with the result that we could not save so much as a mark note or a civilian button. In the next room some one was busy telephoning all details of the affair to the Commandant – occasionally a German passing through the room would stop to look us up and down and call us fools, and an officer asked me with great interest why we had done it.

Only three months – three months' prison pending trial, and then no trial. Bastin to another camp – Duncan and I back to Zorndorf – no prospects and no hope; further in fact than we had ever been before from the thing we wanted most in the world.

Chapter Fifteen

I have to tell now of the most inactive nine months of my captivity. As may (or may not) be generally known, it is against international law to punish an officer prisoner of war with more than fourteen days arrest for an attempted escape, and the Germans had, therefore, brought against us an additional charge of theft, accusing us of having intended to steal the irons which had been used in the construction of the ladder. At the end of three months it had, however, been decided that there was not sufficient evidence of this intention and so we had been returned to the camp. It occurred to us that this charge having fallen through, we were entitled to claim that the time we had spent in gaol should count towards our period of good behaviour. We therefore wrote an official letter on the subject to the General in Command at Küstrin, and to our delight received a favourable reply. This meant that we might hope to leave about August, and we at once set about making preparations for a jump from the train, doing what we could so as to arrange our uniforms that they could be converted into civilians at short notice. To leave Zorndorf came to be our one idea – our one desire in life – and so childishly intent were we on this matter that often I would wake Duncan in the morning, wearing a German cap, and would say, pretending to be one of the orderly room staff:

"Herr Leutnant, Heute kommen sie weg" ("You will leave the fort today,") and he would ask to which camp he was being sent, and receive the most delightful details …

One day I was sent for to the orderly room to be told that proceedings had been taken against me for an affair in which Midi

and I had been caught about five months before. 'We had broken
into the powder-room with the object of starting a tunnel from there
– had picked three locks, and were just at work on the fourth and
last, when we had blundered on an electric alarm, and had been
caught red-handed. I was now told that my court-martial would
take place in July, and that I should remain at Zorndorf until such
time as the whole affair was finished. This was a shocking bad
hearing and I was terribly depressed – not so much so, however, as
when, appearing before court-martial in Berlin, I was sentenced to
eight months' imprisonment for mutiny, conspiracy and attempted
forcible outbreak. I need not say that I availed myself of my right to
appeal, for I could never have reconciled myself to such a sentence,
but I knew that now I was lost and that I should only be transferred
from the fort to prison.

One morning in August the news came that Duncan was to leave
for another camp, and that, I think, was my worst moment since
the time of my capture in France. I scarcely dared to walk about the
fort after he had gone, for everything reminded me most bitterly of
our endless conversations, and of the countless plans we had made
together. Black days! ...

I think of the remainder of my existence there as a grey monotony,
with hardly an incident to distinguish one hateful day from another.
I was to appear before the Court of Appeal in October, but I knew
that no opportunity of escape would be given me, though I almost
welcomed the journey as something to relieve the tedium of my life.
My escort consisted of an officer, a Feldwebel, an under-officer and
a private, and I was most thoroughly searched before leaving the
fort.

On the way to Berlin I asked for permission to visit the lavatory,
for I was anxious to see what precautions were then in vogue. An
order had been previously issued that prisoners were never to be

allowed to shut themselves up in lavatories on the trains, as several had done this, and had then made their escape by the window. I saw the officer catch the Feldwebel's eye as I asked, and they both smiled faintly. Much to my astonishment I was allowed to close the door, and having done so I started to lower the window, making no little noise about it. Outside in the corridor I heard a click, and suddenly opening the door again found that the under-officer had lowered *his* window and that he and the private were waiting with loaded rifles to see me climb out. I gave them a broad grin as I pushed past them and walked back to our own compartment, and as they followed me in, the officer raised his eyebrows questioningly, and the N.C.O. shook his head! The court-martial lasted about two hours and the appeal was dismissed. I was asked if I had anything to say and I spoke for a few minutes in German, telling them that I had seen it stated in a German paper that no prisoner could be punished with more than six weeks' imprisonment for an attempted escape. They informed me that I could make a second and final appeal should I desire to, and one of them muttered that my term of imprisonment was to be served *after the War!* The words were scarcely out of his mouth when he was peremptorily silenced by the President, who then turned to me invitingly, saying:

"You will appeal, yes?"

Had I appealed I should have been kept at Zorndorf until my appearance, perhaps nine months later, before the Supreme Court; had I only nodded my head I should have been a prisoner till the end of the War, but, thank Heaven, I saw the trap and replied emphatically:

"I accept the punishment."

The President turned angrily towards the member who had spoken. "You should not have told him that," he said, and then, "Next case."

But I returned jubilant to the fort, feeling that at last I was delivered from my difficulties and that from now on it was only a matter of days before I should find myself in a new camp.

October passed and then November. A very famous escaper had arrived at Zorndorf.

Captain Cartwright, of the Middlesex Regiment – but though we spent much time together, we were unable to devise any scheme whatever which might lead to freedom. We worked constantly at the fabrication of travelling papers, and I found myself able now to produce rubber stamps which were very much better than anything I had seen before. A certain number of forbidden articles, such as compasses, files, etc., were now being sent out in our parcels, but the censorship over the latter had become so severe that we found it necessary to break into the room where they were kept before distribution, remove such things as we thought might contain *verbotenes* stuff, and make up the weight of the parcel with books. The Germans found that this was being done, and they set about constructing a new parcel room, and meanwhile replaced the padlock on the door of the old room by two new and intricate ones.

The Commandant of the camp had recently had the opportunity of snubbing the prisoners, and I need not say that he had taken advantage of the opportunity. Some Russians had started to saw through the window bars in the chapel, but this being discovered the Commandant had had a label affixed to the bars with the word "Zwecklos" ("useless") written upon it, followed by his signature and the orderly room stamp.

One night Cartwright and myself, having prepared a label the exact replica of the one I have just described, and ornamented it with an exact reproduction of the orderly room stamp, which I myself had made, went down to the parcel room. We managed to pick both the locks, and on the lamp hung in the centre of the room we hung our skeleton keys with the label attached. We locked the doors again behind us, for the padlocks were of the spring type which clip on, and left the Germans to discover our little witticism in the morning – feeling that we were one up on them!

About this time there began to be a certain amount of discussion over the question of interning in Holland all officers who had been more than three years in captivity, but not a few of us regarded this prospect with horror. We were in fact absolutely determined that nothing should induce us to go, for once in Holland one lost all right to attempt escape, and we felt that our only hope of future happiness lay in freeing ourselves before the end. Some time in January, 1918, we received information that our Government allowed each individual to exercise his own discretion as to whether he should go or not, and therefore, when the Germans offered me the choice, I elected to remain. This was tantamount to an open confession of my intentions, and I imagine that I should have been detained at Zorndorf for the duration of the War but for a visit made to the camp by the Dutch Ambassador. The Germans had agreed that no prisoner should ever be kept in the camp for more than eight months, and the moment they heard that His Excellency was coming they decided to evacuate me (for I had been there a year and a half), and I was informed that I must prepare to leave at short notice.

It is impossible for me to exaggerate the joy I felt at this news. I had grown almost accustomed to the idea of finding myself a prisoner at the end of it all – almost reconciled to the loss of everything I valued – almost resigned to starting life again far away from every one I had known. And now it was all changed and I had still a chance.

Oh, Zorndorf! I see you again as I left you – grassy mounds and winding paths – spiked railings and monstrous walls – dark passages, scowling sentries, and the clash of arms. You very nearly broke me, but you didn't quite!

Chapter Sixteen

"Hullo, Hardy, I've been waiting six weeks for the likes of you. You're for it, of course?"

I was standing by my baggage outside the orderly room of Schweidnitz camp, and the speaker was Captain Willie Loder-Symonds. of the Wiltshire Regiment – a man of about ten years' service who had been wounded and taken during the Mons retreat, and whom I had met in my first camp. He had grown a beard and looked much older than when I had first known him, but his red face and thick neck and his enormous shoulders were unmistakable, and I was delighted to see him again.

"Of *course* I'm for it," I said. "Anything doing?"

"Anything *doing?* The easiest thing you ever had in your life! You'll spot it if you walk round the camp a couple of times."

"Right," said I. "Got a typewriter?"

"I can get one."

"Can you get me an old rubber shoe sole?" I asked.

"You bet. I can get civvies too."

"Well, I've got ninety marks soldered up in a tin of milk," I said. "Have you got any?"

"About a hundred and fifty," replied Loder.

"Home in a fortnight then, old skin," said I, and we both laughed.

I was not able to go at once with him to his room, for I was obliged to wait until my particulars had been taken and my baggage searched, and it was an hour before this was finished. There was, Loder had told me, scarcely another man in the camp whom I knew, and I did not therefore waste much time, after finding to which room I had been posted, before setting off for a tour of inspection.

The camp had once been a workhouse and did not appear by any means an uncomfortable place. It was simply a large courtyard containing a number of buildings and huts, and surrounded by a ten foot brick wall topped with broken glass. This wall formed the outer defence of the camp, and prisoners were prevented from approaching it by means of a wire fence erected at varying distances from it; but the neutral zone was at no point less than five yards deep. There was an unpleasantly large number of sentries posted about, and stands for the latter had been built on top of the wall, but none of these things represented to the average prisoner so great an obstacle as the four hundred and fifty miles which lay between Schweidnitz and the Dutch frontier.

I had not walked more than twice round the camp before I saw what I imagined to be the weak spot to which Loder had referred. There was a stretch of wall about seventy yards long which formed one end of the camp, and here also was the usual wire fence. A sentry stand had been erected on the wall at one end, and there were in addition two sentries on our side of the wire, responsible for seeing that no one entered the neutral zone. In our favour were two things. A long hut had been built parallel to and very near the wire, and the sentries were in the habit of sometimes walking round the hut, on which occasions one had only to reckon with the man mounted on the stand. The second point which drew my attention was that several small plum trees grew against the wall, and, though they were very flimsy, it was certain that they would be of great help in scaling it.

Delighted though I was at what I had seen, I thought it as well to continue my examination in case I should find something better, but finished up very much in favour of an attempt at the place I have described, so I went off in search of Loder.

He was waiting for me in his room, and he proceeded at once to describe such details of the camp as affected us. He told me that it had been open for about five months, but that hitherto no attempt to escape had been made – a point immensely in our favour. The majority of the prisoners were flying men, but there were a number of merchant skippers and ships' officers there who had been captured by the the U boats, and many of them wore civilian clothes. Loder was very popular with most of these men, and he did not doubt, he said, that they would give us all we needed in the way of mufti. A tunnel was in progress and, though he did not believe that it was anywhere near completion, he thought we should not delay a single day more than was necessary. If accomplices were needed, Loder could get them; if a typewriter was required, Loder could have it there tomorrow; and if I could only guarantee to take him through Germany and dump him five miles from the frontier he could in turn promise to take me over it, without my having even to think for myself. And on the bargain we shook hands laughingly.

I had heard constantly of Loder's efforts during the previous two years, and I knew that he had escaped from Burg some months before, and had travelled as far as Aachen in the train with a Russian who spoke German. Aachen lies only about four miles from the Dutch frontier but, being a very large town, the supervision of papers in the station was not very severe, and Loder had succeeded in leaving the town with his companion, but had been arrested on the frontier. He had unwisely attempted to cross by day and, though this had been the probable cause of his failure, it had enabled him to acquaint himself with the dispositions of sentries there. I had the greatest confidence in his skill and courage, for he had given proof of them in all his attempts, and his name had become a byword for daring and determination. The fact that he spoke so little German as to make it unsafe for him to open his mouth during a journey did not trouble us, for I felt myself quite capable of doing the talking for both. I might incidentally record the curious fact that from the moment of meeting each other at Schweidnitz we both felt that the hour of our freedom was near, and that this might be the last stunt.

We began now to discuss the actual breakout, and were of one accord in thinking that the side which I have described offered the greatest possibilities. It would of course be necessary to make the attempt after dark for, though the camp was brightly illumined, the wall would cast a heavy shadow on the far side, and this was very essential to us in order that we should not be seen by the man on the stand as we walked away. We also decided that we should need accomplices to engage the attention of the two sentries as we crossed the neutral zone and climbed the wall, but this could be easily arranged for.

While I was walking about that afternoon I saw a German civilian, who was, I was told, the photographer who visited the camp once a week. I ran off at once to tell Loder and, having borrowed a British warm, and removed the shoulder straps which gave it a military appearance, I went out and asked to be photographed. The German was, of course, forbidden to take a prisoner in anything except uniform, but he had no hesitation in photographing me as I was then. Loder arrived a few moments later, dressed as I was, but wearing a pair of spectacles with lenses of such strength that he was unable to see where he was going, and his eyes looked horribly distorted through them. I was in fits of laughter as he stood there looking like the caricature of a German, with cropped head and pointed beard, but the photographer took him quite seriously and did not so much as smile. We were told the photos would be ready in a week, and I therefore decided that it would be as well to get to work on the papers immediately.

Neither of us had ever yet seen a real passport, and it was highly probable that the formula I was using was nothing approaching the authentic one. I overcame this difficulty by typing at the top of the paper the words "Temporary Pass," and added a small note to the effect that the permanent pass had been recalled for verification. I then wrote an exact description of myself, stating that I was lame and blind in one eye and that I was a baker's apprentice. This paper was supposed to have been issued by the Aachen police, and I intended to show it should it be necessary in the early stages of our journey. It is obvious that I would not dare to show such a pass in or near Aachen, for the police there would be well acquainted with their own stamps, etc., and I therefore made out another, purporting to be issued by the Schweidnitz police, for use in Western Germany. I then made out a small slip on which I typed a few sentences granting me permission to travel from Aachen to Schweidnitz and back, and another permitting me to travel from Schweidnitz to Aachen and back. It will, therefore, be seen that, if arrested in Western Germany, I should produce the Schweidnitz pass and the permit to visit Aachen, while if stopped at the beginning, I should show the Aachen pass and the paper which would account for our presence in Eastern Germany. The ruse was of Loder's conception and was invaluable to us.

I had now to start on the stamps, of which I should need two. Loder had provided me with a piece of rubber and a pair of compasses, and I worked practically without a break for three days, and produced a result which I could scarcely believe was of my doing. I remember the moment when, having finished the first, which bore the German eagle in a double circle surrounded by the words "Polizei Verwaltung der Stadt Aachen", and having prepared some ink on a small pad, I made a trial impression. Loder stood looking anxiously over my shoulder as I pressed the stamp down, and I hardly dared to raise it from the paper, fearing to find that it had left nothing but a blurred and inky smudge. And then I lifted it, and we both whistled.

"Not only is it precisely like a stamp," said Loder, "but it's like a brand new one."

And this was almost a fact, for every feather on the eagle showed, the circles were clear and regular, and the lettering surprisingly distinct – all very trivial, I suppose, but the best piece of work I ever did!

The second stamp was finished by the time the photos were ready. The latter were obviously, to an Englishman, those of officers in British uniform, but it was quite conceivable that they would deceive the Germans, for the Germans never succeeded in reconciling themselves to the idea of a collar and tie with fighting kit. We gummed the photos on to our papers (I had made a complete set for Loder, describing him as a baker), and we then impressed the stamp across the edge of the print in the usual manner, and also stamped the papers at the top. The travelling permits had to be treated in the same way, and when this was done we each bought a small wallet at the canteen and carried our passes about in them, ready to be destroyed in case of emergency.

I had been eight days in the camp before all this was finished, and it was now the 27th of February, 1918. We chose the 1st of March as the date of our escape, and the hour seven o'clock in the evening, that is to say, about a quarter of an hour after evening roll call. We had heard that a train left for Dresden about 9.30 p.m., and we hoped to catch this one, should the break out be successful. The Germans were certain to have retained a couple of prints of our photographs, and we realized that these would be circulated within a very short time of our absence becoming known. It was essential, therefore, that we should be well on our way before morning roll call which, being held outside, would be very difficult, if not impossible, to fake.

We arranged with an Englishman who spoke German that he should engage one of the sentries in conversation while we were making the attempt, and we also enlisted the services of a British orderly who, armed with a ham sandwich, was to lure the other round the hut. We should be obliged to wear our military greatcoats and caps while walking from our rooms to the wall, for we should have to pass many sentries, and we therefore arranged with a Canadian officer – a splendid man who had come with me from Zorndorf – that he should hand us our civilian coats through the bars of one of the hut windows. Whilst Loder scaled the wall I was to take these and throw them over it, and was then to hand our uniform stuff to the Canadian, who would close the window and carry everything back to our rooms. In this way we hoped to get clear without leaving a single trace behind us.

We bought a sausage at the canteen and this, with the small amount of chocolate which we both had, was all we intended to carry. Loder had arranged with two ships' officers to exchange their civilian clothes for our uniforms, and the idea that this might incriminate them after our escape did not appear to trouble them in the slightest. We neither intended to wear jackets, for we could not afford to be hampered in climbing the wall; but the lack of them could easily be hidden by wearing our overcoats buttoned up. We had also the good fortune to obtain two Homburg hats – a very necessary part of our equipment, for caps had come to be regarded with suspicion in Germany, as they were invariably worn by escaping prisoners. We had no map, and Loder assured me that we should need none, but I had concealed a compass in the back of a clothes brush, having split the wood, hollowed out a space sufficiently large to contain the instrument, and then glued the two pieces together again. We both carried pen knives, and I had retempered the blade of mine and made a saw edge on it, my idea being that, should we be retaken

I Escape!   145

and locked up, I might be able to cut through the bars of my cell and so escape again. It did not seem to me probable that, even should we be arrested, the Germans would deprive me of the brush, which looked innocent in the extreme. We had borrowed a cushion with which to cover the broken glass on the wall and so protect ourselves, and we had also obtained a walking stick. One of the skippers had unhesitatingly given us his watch as soon as he heard the purpose for which we needed it, and we promised to send it to his wife if we got home, which promise we kept.

Although, as I have said, we both felt assured of ultimate success, these impressions do not of course remain continuously with a man. Loder and I realized well the seriousness of the position in which we found ourselves, for, though he had hitherto avoided being sent to Zorndorf, we knew now that another failure would inevitably lead to our internment there till the end of the War. We were desperate, and we even went to the extent of swearing solemnly that, once up on the wall, we would drop, no matter what the height be, nor what there were upon the other side.

We dressed in Loder's room about an hour before roll call on the evening of the 1st of March and got all our things ready. We divided up our money in case one or other of us should be taken, and we carried our sets of papers apart, so that there might be no confusion. As far as Hanover we were, we decided, to be Aachen men, and from there on were to state that we lived at Schweidnitz.

We got into civilians and, pulling our khaki slacks over our black trousers, appeared on parade in greatcoats. By the time roll call was over it was dark, and the lights were turned on, but we thought ourselves safe in removing our khaki trousers, for there were many civilians in the camp and we felt that our military greatcoats would prevent any suspicion being aroused. We then filled our pockets with the food we were taking; Loder took his spectacles and some soap, I my brush and a razor, and we were prepared!

The accomplices were already in position as we walked out, and though we spoke no word to them they knew precisely how to act. We were to walk to the other side of the camp and then back, by which time both sentries were to be on the far side of the hut. The orderly would, it had been arranged, go into the building to fetch another sandwich while the sentry waited, and the officer was of opinion that he would be able to engage his man for about two minutes – and no longer, for his stock of German words was very limited. Should the sentry on the stand see us we were done, but of this we had to take the risk and think ourselves lucky that it was no worse.

As we walked on our return journey towards the wall I felt myself almost choking nth excitement. We pretended to be talking and laughed as we passed groups of prisoners, but I think there was little real mirth left in either of us at that moment. If we failed – if we *failed!* We mustn't dream of it; the thing was unthinkable – we were going Home!

We had passed the end of the hut, and had now turned the corner. We walked on about ten yards and then Loder suddenly flung off his coat and started to climb the wire fence, while I looked anxiously from left to right. Not a sentry was in sight with the exception of the man on the stand, but the wall looked positively white in the blaze of the arc-lamps, and I cursed those lamps, fearing they would prove our downfall yet. A window behind me opened, and the Canadian threw out our coats on to the ground. I leapt to pick them up, and in an instant had flung them clear over the wall and was tearing off the one I wore. I thrust the collar of it through the bars and my friend dragged it through, and Loder's after it.

"Good luck!" he whispered.

"Goodbye and good luck," said I, and then quoting from a song we were both very fond of: "I'm going way back home to have a wonderful time!"

I heard him laugh as he closed the window with a click, and then, turning, I found that Loder had reached the top of the wall and was endeavouring to swing his legs across before dropping on the other side. I had crossed the wire and the instant his hands disappeared I gripped a branch of the little tree and started to climb. I felt it lean from the wall as I mounted, for Loder's weight had torn away the fastenings, and during one dreadful moment I feared that it would crash with me to the ground. But it was growing wood and tough, and it held long enough to enable me to grip the stone coping. A heave – and my elbows were up; another – and I was kneeling on the cushion while the glass crackled under me, and below me Loder whispered: "Drop – drop, you're all right."

It seemed to me as though I spent minutes in getting my legs clear of the glass, but at last I hung by one hand, reached for the cushion with the other, and then let go. I felt as though I should never hit the ground, but when I landed it was upon a heap of leaf manure, and I was not even jolted. Loder had collected the coats and, keeping close within the shadow of the wall, we crept away.

Chapter Seventeen

We were, we knew, in the grounds of a military hospital, and descending a steep hill were not surprised to find our exit barred by a high wire fence and a locked gate. Beyond the fence was a narrow strip of ground, and then came the canal, but we thought we should be able to walk along here until we reached the bridge. We were obliged to wait some time, for there were many couples passing along the canal bank, but at last our opportunity came and we climbed the fence. In doing so I knocked my hat off against the branch of a tree, and found to my horror, on searching for it in the grass, that it had fallen into the water and sunk. Loder had joined me and I said: "I've done it, old boy; my hat's gone." There was a short pause in which we stood there thinking, and then he said:

"Well, take mine, and go and buy another in the town. I'll wait here for you."

I took it, and he lay down in the long grass where he could not be easily seen, and then, hating though I did to leave him there with no hat, and no means of accounting for himself should he be challenged, I set off along the canal bank for the town.

I had walked for half an hour and had lost all sense of direction by the time I reached the shopping district, and here I stopped an old woman and asked her if she could direct me to the nearest hat shop. She told me that there was one in the next street, and so delighted was I that I presented her with a cake of soap and then hurried away without even waiting for her thanks. I was afraid that I might be asked for a permit, it being forbidden in many parts of Germany to sell anything made of cloth except against a *Bezugschein*, but nothing of the sort was demanded and I bought a very smart Homburg for eight marks. It was now a quarter to nine, and it became apparent to me that we should miss the train, which would mean waiting until after eleven. I had the greatest difficulty in finding my way back, and was at last obliged to ask a man whether he could direct me to the prisoner's camp, adding that I was the new interpreter. He showed me the way, and once I saw the lights of the lager ahead of me I knew where I was, and succeeded in reaching the canal bank. Along here I ran at full speed, and Loder, hearing me coming, and seeing in the moonlight that I carried a paper bag, knew that my mission had been successful, and rose, beaming, from the grass. He put on his hat, fixed his spectacles to his satisfaction, and we then set off for the station.

We had missed the 9.30 train, but we thought it as well to buy our tickets at once, for they would serve to substantiate our story should we be challenged while waiting for the next. We went together to the booking office, and I took my place in the queue, for there were a number of people in the station.

As my turn drew near I got our travelling permits ready, and when the clerk asked me for our papers I produced these.

"No," he said, after reading them through, "these are no use. Where are the others?"

I handed him our identity papers, but he still shook his head.

"These won't help you," he said, "they're only permits."

I was utterly flabbergasted, and could not imagine what he wanted.

"What on earth am I to do then? "I asked. "I've simply *got* to get to Leipzig."

"Well, you'll have to pay the full amount," came the answer.

Oh, what a colossal relief! As if I cared what we paid! He had expected us to have half-fare vouchers, thinking we were munition workers, and all my fears had been unfounded. He handed us our fourth class tickets to Leipzig as soon as I produced the money, and we walked out of the station with our heads in the clouds.

We spent an hour tramping up and down the streets and never rested for a moment, knowing as we did that the police are always suspicious of loiterers. Something drew us towards the camp, and we walked round it once or twice, examining the place curiously. From the outside the walls looked very high, and the sentries on their stands gave it the appearance of a convicts' prison; there was something frightening about the realization that, two short hours before, we had been inmates of the place. Half past ten – time we got back to the station. Goodbye, Schweidnitz – goodbye and good luck, you other poor prisoners – goodbye, captivity!

I chatted steadily in German to Loder as we strolled about on the platform, smoking cigarettes and waiting for our train. He knew enough of the language to understand me when I spoke slowly, and this saved me from the trouble of taking him aside when I wished to explain anything. We got into an empty fourth class compartment, and were able in consequence to talk English until arriving at Liegnitz, where we had to change. From then on we travelled in a crowd, and pretended to be asleep most of the time. Occasionally I would see Loder push up his spectacles on to his forehead in an effort to ease his eyes, but my dreadful frowns always induced him to lower them again. I noticed that his eyes were becoming very bloodshot, and he told me afterwards that his head ached furiously the whole time, but this was as nothing to him compared with the horror of recapture.

It was four o'clock in the morning before we reached Dresden, and here we found to our disgust that we should be obliged to wait about three hours for the Leipzig train, unless we cared to travel by express. Express trains contained no fourth class carriages and the police supervision of second and third-class passengers was very severe, but we decided nevertheless that we could not afford to wait.

We accordingly got into a crowded compartment and, sure enough, had not travelled ten miles before the door was slid open, and a man shouted:

"All papers ready, please!"

He produced his own for the purpose of satisfying us that he was an agent of police, and he then stretched out his hand for mine, for I sat next to the door. With fear and trembling I reached them out to him, and he turned with them towards the light and started to read. I studied every expression of his face as he did so, and when he began to examine the stamp my heart sank within me.

"Where is your military-free paper? "he asked.

"I haven't got it with me," I replied. "But it's obvious that they would not have issued me with a travelling permit if I was liable for service."

"That's so," he said, and, handing my passports back to me, turned to my next door neighbour.

I looked across at Loder and raised my hand to my face to hide my delighted grins.

I was on the qui vive in case he too should be questioned, and was prepared to interfere at once, but his papers were considered quite satisfactory, and the policeman even remarked that he wished all were as clear and concise as ours!

On arriving at Leipzig we went out into the town and bought some cigarettes. It was two years since I had been here, but I had unpleasant recollections of the railway station and did not care to remain there longer than was absolutely necessary. We returned a quarter of an hour before our train left, and bought tickets right through to Cologne, but these I purchased at separate booking offices, for I did not like to display so much money at one time. The

train left at about 11 a.m., and we felt that we were keeping well
ahead of any possible pursuit, and that we had little more to fear
until we reached the frontier.

Our journey between Leipzig and Cologne was a very long and
tiring one. Loder and I were lucky to have one seat between us,
and we took it in turns to stand, but were very often both on our
feet for hours on end, having given up the seat to a woman. Papers
were examined as we drew near Hanover, but ours were accepted
without a word and we were not troubled again. We occasionally
dived into our pockets and fished out small pieces of chocolate, but
these we were obliged to eat surreptitiously, though we made a great
show of our sausage and slices of German bread. It was nine o'clock
before we reached Cologne, to find that we had two hours to wait
for the Aachen train. We were both very dirty and uncomfortable,
so we made our way to a lavatory, where we shaved and washed.
We entered separate compartments, and after a short time I heard
muffled growls from Loder, among which I distinguished the word
"Seife". I threw the soap over the partition and then waited until
he had finished shaving and could let me have the razor. We then
bought tickets to Aachen and walked out into the town, but feeling
very cold and miserable we entered a restaurant and ordered some
soup. This place was altogether too fashionable for people dressed
like ourselves, and many of the guests looked at us curiously, while
the waitress treated us with undisguised contempt. My stock of
conversation was running low, and we did not feel easy until we had
finished our soup and sallied once more into the street. For some
time we strolled about in the dark and then returned to the station;
fortunately well in time for the train, for never before have I seen
so crowded a station. We were among the first into our carriage,
but had to get up at once to give our seat to two girls. The carriage
was intended to hold eighteen, but there were between fifty and

sixty packed into it before we moved off, and one became quite accustomed to the piteous cry: "Tür nicht aufmachen, sonst falle ich heraus" ("Don't open the door or I shall fall out").

We had travelled in this state for about fifteen minutes when Loder, who stood beside me, suddenly started to cough and whispered to me that he was fainting. I looked up and found him as white as a sheet, and was not altogether surprised, for he had soldiered abroad for several years and was, I knew, subject to attacks of malaria. There was some slight satisfaction to be gained from the fact that we were packed too tightly for it to be possible for him to fall, so I left him where he was and started to fight my way towards the lavatory. Others pushed him along behind me and at last we got him in, and, lowering the window, pushed his head out. He seemed very bad, and for a short time I feared that that he would be unable to carry on, but by the time we reached Aachen he was much better.

The sight of the enormous crowd at the barrier there assured me that we had nothing to fear in the way of supervision of papers, and we found ourselves before long in the darkened streets. It was now midnight and we had a certain five hours of darkness in which to cover the few miles which lay between us and the frontier. I made Loder a little bow and said:

"There's my part done. The rest is up to you, and I'm only a passenger."

"That's all you need to be," he answered. "This is my show."

He appeared indeed to know the way well, and, though it was over a year since he had been in Aachen, he remembered the smallest details and was able to tell me exactly what turnings we should pass and which bridges we had to cross. A tram passed going in the direction of Richtericht and we boarded it, and thus saved ourselves two miles of tramping. Getting off just before reaching the last named place, we walked back a short distance in the direction from which we had come and then suddenly leaving the road started to cross through rough and broken country. I had no idea where we were going, but followed Loder blindly, for I had the most perfect confidence in his word that he could, and would, fulfil his part of the contract.

We reached a railway cutting which Loder believed to be patrolled, and we descended into it with the greatest caution, crossed the lines, and then, having climbed the other bank, ran for some distance. We were circling all the time to the right in an effort to strike a road of which Loder knew, and which would give him his direction, and this road we at last found after some time of anxious wandering. From then we pushed on steadily, keeping the road always in sight, and the fact that every hedge was wired showed us that we were very near our goal. We saw several sentries and had constantly to crawl for long distances, and the state of our clothes can be well imagined, for it had been raining. We eventually found ourselves plodding wearily through heavy plough land, and often we would seize each other by the arm at the sight of a sentry, who turned out more than once to be merely the stump of a tree. We were both very, very tired, and at last, seeing a small group of houses ahead of us, decided to approach them in the hope of finding something which might tell us where we were.

Every window was dark and not so much as the bark of a dog was to be heard as we tiptoed through that tiny village of whitewashed houses, and we were almost abreast of the last building, when we heard behind us the clatter of heavy boots on the hard road, and a voice cried:

"Halt!"

"Don't run! don't run!" Loder whispered, and we turned to find two soldiers unslinging their rifles. In the dark it was impossible to see their uniforms and we walked slowly towards them, determined if they were Germans to put them off their guard and then attack them. I say this in no boastful spirit, but we were desperate, and after all, I thought, Loder was a match for any two!

Speaking in German, I called out:

"Look here, we are Dutch, and we have crossed into Germany by accident – can you show us our way back?"

There was a pause, and then one of them replied in broken German:

"I don't understand."

Scarcely able to believe our ears, scarcely able to breathe for the hammering of our hearts, we approached still nearer, and suddenly Loder shouted at the top of his voice:

"By God! They're Dutchmen!"

"Dutchmen? "I said stupidly. "But, if that's so, we must be in Holland."

"We are, old thing," said he.

And then, in the slowest and most precise German, I started to tell them that we were two escaped British officers, and I asked them whether we were far over the frontier. They were all smiles now and told us that we were fifty yards over the border, and, pointing to a light about a hundred yards away, explained that the house from which it shone stood on German soil. Loder was dancing in the road like a crazy creature, and I – well, I just stood there and tried to realize it.

Three and a half years – three and a half years of misery and shame and bitter disappointment – three and a half years of straining after a thing one longed for, and that seemed as though one were never to grasp, and now one's hand closed over it and the years fell back like a dream.

"Look here, Loder," I said, "let's get this to rights. Two days ago we were prisoners at Schweidnitz and now we're free. *Is that so?*"

But Loder had walked down the road with one of the sentries to see the actual frontier, so I sat down at the side of the road with my head in my hands to wait till he came back.

Oh, my readers, I wonder if any one of you have ever known such joy as I felt, sitting there in the dark. Were I never to know again the meaning of ease, and were I doomed for ever to sorrow and catastrophe, I say that I had had more than my share of happiness in life – that nothing else in life can ever stir me again as I was stirred then . . .

"Souvenir?" said the sentry eagerly.

We spent the night at a little inn in the village, and everybody was kindness itself. We promised five pounds to each of the sentries and they seemed very gratified, and felt no doubt that they had done a good night's work.

Whether the inn was full, or whether our appearance was not such as to justify the proprietor in trusting us between his sheets, I do not know; but, be that as it may, we spent the night on benches in the bar parlour, and wakened in the morning to a splendid breakfast of ham and eggs. We were supplied with a guide to take us to the nearest railway station, but we took every precaution to see that he did not lead us back into Germany. Such things have happened before now, and our man spoke unpleasantly fluent German, but be it to his credit that he led us straight and was well paid for his trouble.

I cannot describe how strange it felt to sit there in the train, with a copy of "Punch" in one's hand, and talking English as though one were at home. It had been worth while, we agreed, whatever the future might hold for us.

Had we known what fate, in dealing us liberty with one hand, was preparing to deal us with the other, we should not have grumbled. Had Loder had any foreboding of that moment, ten weeks later, that was to send him crashing to earth – dead, beneath the debris of a wrecked machine, would he have forgone that hour upon the frontier and all that went before? I knew him well, and I say a hundred times, no!

On arriving at Maastricht we took a cab to the British Consulate, but finding the Consul away were obliged to visit his Belgian confrère, and here we experienced a most kind reception. We were taken to a shop and fitted out with civilian clothes, for which no payment was asked, and we were invited to lunch, and given more champagne than was good for us. That afternoon we travelled to Rotterdam and this time found ourselves expected at the Consulate. They were all very good to us indeed, patted us on the back and then gave us twenty five pounds apiece to amuse ourselves with; and having photographed us for the necessary passports and warned us to reappear in three days, they sent us up to the Hague, where a number of our friends were interned.

We went on board our ship on the 5th of March, and though the convoy did not sail for nearly a week we were not allowed ashore again. The ghastly possibility of the convoy being attacked was ever present in our minds, and we often pictured ourselves arriving in Bremerhaven in a German destroyer. We ran into a thick fog in the North Sea, and it was found necessary to tow a keg behind us in order to show our position to the ship following us. The keg went adrift, and this fact gave rise to a certain amount of shouting and hurried orders, with the result that Loder and myself – who were both totally ignorant.

In the village you stop a young subaltern whom you seem to know, and you say, proud at remembering his name:

"Hullo, Harry. You haven't aged a day."

"I'm not Harry," he answers, apparently slightly annoyed, "Harry was killed on the Somme. I'm the baby of the family, you know. You wouldn't remember me."

At the door you are greeted sedately by the same old cocker, who never thought of you as anything but his equal, and you notice that the "begging" patches on his stern are worn a little bit balder than when you knew him last. In your room everything is as you left it – nothing changed but yon. And all the time something is welling up in you, but you don't know what it is. Lord! how queer – how queer …

And then came the orders for Loder and myself to be present on a certain day at Buckingham Palace, and we were each alone for some time with the King. No one could have been kinder or more sympathetic than he was, and in the honour done us by this interview we felt we gained a great reward.

For the rest there is little to tell. Loder's sad death I have already indicated. Baschwitz after his escape had joined the British Intelligence Service and on my return to London we had a joyous reunion. He was on the eve of a fearful adventure, for in April, 1918, he crossed the lines in a small balloon and, coming down in German territory, spent six months there among the enemy – organizing espionage. For this terribly dangerous work he was awarded the D.S.O.

As for myself, it would have been too much to expect that I should come scatheless to the end of the War. I was in the line six months and took part in several actions; but the Germans had the last word, for five weeks from the finish I was back again in England with a bullet in my tummy and a leg left behind me in France.

THE END